PUZZLE PALACE

THE BOY WHO WOULD BE GENERAL:
AN ODYSSEY OF MANIC PSYCHOSIS

SGT KEVIN JOHN KELLER USAF (RET.)

100% DISABLED AMERICAN VETERAN

iUniverse, Inc.

New York   Bloomington

PUZZLE PALACE
THE BOY WHO WOULD BE GENERAL:
AN ODYSSEY OF MANIC PSYCHOSIS

iUniverse books may be ordered through booksellers or by contacting:

iUniverse
1663 Liberty Drive
Bloomington, IN 47403
www.iuniverse.com
1-800-Authors (1-800-288-4677)

Because of the dynamic nature of the Internet, any Web addresses or links contained in this book may have changed since publication and may no longer be valid. The views expressed in this work are solely those of the author and do not necessarily reflect the views of the publisher, and the publisher hereby disclaims any responsibility for them.

ISBN: 978-1-4401-3160-8 (sc)
ISBN: 978-1-4401-3161-5 (ebook)

Printed in the United States of America

iUniverse rev. date: 3/31/09

This book is dedicated to the Late Arthur John Keller, my father, and Helen Marie Keller, my mother, and my golf coach "Craig" of Shelby Oaks Golf Club, the best golf club on the planet

Acknowledgement:

Dr Walters Dayton VA Medical Center, the best shrink on the living bio-mass called "Mother Earth", and Dr Rhee, and Dr Lee; Psych Nurses Jackie, Dorothy Brown, and Tina, and Fr Gerry Pastor of Holy Angels, Fr Patrick Associate Pastor and Deacon John, and to Mercedes my therapist, and to my best friend Theresa for all her love and support, and my dear friend and former director of Veteran's House, Audrey, and to my sons, Daniel and David, and to my daughter Chrissie where ever she may be on the planet, and my brother Douglas, sisters Ellen and Maryann, Mike Martin my VA social worker, and to Ed Ball of the Sidney VA Office, and Jack the Van Driver, Mr. and Mrs. Martino

Kaitlyn of iUNIVERSE, and to Sheriff Kevin O'Leary: "Work on that book!

Chief Wearly: Chief of Sidney Police for his kind words

Karen of the Sidney "Chase Bank" for putting up with me

Gordon Bailey former Landlord at North Main

Nickie Landlord at Towne Centre Apartments

Tharon of Solar Systems for my new 3.4 gig hertz duo core system unit

Karen and all my friends at the Sidney "Alcove"

and Sidney "Spot Café": Holley, Caroline, Nancy, Carolyn

and Sidney "In Good Taste" and Sidney "Lee's Chinese",

most of all I wish to thank the kind and good people of Sidney

for their emotional support, and for their warmth and friendliness,

And all the wonderful staff of the Dayton VA Medical Center

And to the memory of the Late General Huyser and wonderful commander and boss

"THOSE WHO FORGET THE PAST
ARE DOOMED TO REPEAT IT"
author unknown

"Mother is the name for God
on the lips of children all over the world",
from the movie "The Crow"

The Puzzle Palace Community: All entries to the community will have a personal, private and highly confidential reply

Within 24 hours: <u>kevin_keller01@yahoo.com</u>

Belief System: "One Globe, One Race, One Peace of Mind"
Kevin John Paul Keller July 2003

BOOK ONE

Preface

The author of this surrealistic prose narrative attempts to capture the soul's quest to find self amidst the torrent and mindscape of manic psychosis…this subjective mindscape of soul struggles to cope with the debasement…defilement… disaffirmation…depreciation and emotional devastation of the true sarcoma …of our culture…divorce

Homeless…wandering the toxic street water wasteland …lost now to the undertow of manic psychosis, the soul seeks to affirm itself. He finds himself seeking a way back home to the father's house, that at 19 yrs of age, he left in pained rejection The title of this work reflects a 92 day isolation at a city jail in Virginia for sending flowers to "Cris" after a Judge ordered no contact.   This contempt of court violation was further compounded due to my manic psychosis as an inmate of this jail. Names have been changed in this text to protect privacy.

This psychoanalytical journal runs from February 1989 to January 2009. It reflects the trauma of Bi-Polar disorder. It is the author's hope the public will gain insight on this disorder in this reading. Today this disorder is not well reflected in the media which would have us believe that every gunman with a desire to kill is Bi-Polar. This is not the case. Many people with Bi-Polar disorder have no such intent. Violent behavior is the last thing on their mind. As reflected in these pages they struggle with their emotions. This is a mood disorder, of the emotions.

The author offers no apologies for his use of the name " Silver Fox" for his best friend and Divine Father.

POSTINGS:

MEDICAL CENTERS ATTENDED AS INPATIENT FOR MANIC PSYCHOSIS

1980   Jefferson Barracks VA Medical Center
1981   Malcolm Grow Air Force Medical Center, Andrews AFB Washington D.C.
1982   Hampton VA Medical Center, Hampton Virginia
1992   Dayton VA Medical Center, Dayton Ohio
1994   Roanoke VA Medical Center, Roanoke Virginia
1994   San Antonio VA Medical Center, San Antonio, Texas
1994   La Rosa Private Medical Center, San Antonio, Texas
1994   Wright-Patterson Air Force Base Medical Center, Fairborn, Ohio
1995   Albany VA Medical Center, Albany New York
2004   Dayton VA Medical Center, Dayton Ohio
2005   Northport VA Medical Center, Northport New York

GROUP HOMES

1993   San Antonio Group Home, Texas
1995   "Sunken Meadows" Northport New York
1998   "Hope House" Fairborn, Ohio
1998   "Veteran's House" Sidney Ohio to 2003
2004   Private Group Home Residence

POSTINGS

Sidney Daily News Friday, July 18, 2003

LOCAL-REGION
"Writing from the Heart": Man recounts rise and fall in the Air Force. Page 1B

SIDNEY RESIDENT WRITES BOOK ABOUT DEALING
WITH MANIC PSYCHOSIS
By Michael Everman
Staff Writer
meverman@sdccg.com

"The Boy Who Would Be General: An Odyssey of Manic Psychosis" is the story of a local man's rapid promotion through the ranks of the U.S. Air Force, which one day led him to break down and lose contact with reality. The book also recounts how he has spent the remainder of his life dealing with his manic psychosis. Retired Sgt Kevin Keller of Sidney was one of the select few to be chosen as member of the Air Force Elite Guard of Scott Air Force Base in Belleville Ill, during the Iranian Crisis of 1979.

As a member of the elite guard, it was his job to protect the command headquarters of the base and serve as a body guard for the commanding staff, Keller said. The commanding staff included the four star General Huyser, three star General Ryan, 2 star General Block, 1 star General Braingshi.. Huyser had to be guarded 24 hours a day, seven days a week, due to threats against his life, Keller said. This was because Huyser was instrumental in flying the Shah of Iran, Mohammed Reeza Pahlavi, out of his country once an opposition movement overthrew him in 1979.

The Shite Muslims took over the country and wanted Huyser dead after he helped the shah, Keller said. They saw him as a Christian and Western Force who invaded their country. My job as a member of the elite guard was to keep Huyser safe and make sure there was never a terrorist penetration at the base. It was a job he loved and took seriously. I totally ate it up, Keller said about his experience in the Air Force. I loved every minute of it. However it was his love for the Air Force that eventually led to the end of his military career and years of mental instability I was working 18 to 20 hrs a day Keller said. I drove myself to the breaking point. The breaking point came around Labor Day 1980. A few days before, he severely reprimanded one of his troops for messing up at his post. Keller said. I was trying to show my authority so I made an example out him in front of the entire flight crew. He said. I was a new sergeant, so I wanted to be tough. However reprimanding the airman had the complete adverse effect on him later. A few days later, the airman who had broken up with is longtime girlfriend got drunk and committed suicide crashing his car into a tractor-trailer at around 100 mph, Keller said.. Keller's police commander called him into his office the next day and showed him the photo's of the man's mangled body. " I freaked out because they were so disturbing", Keller said. " I blamed myself for him killing himself." During this time Keller was supposed to be taking a leave of absence because he was preparing to enter officer training school in Texas. " I was determined to be a general one day", Keller said "If I'd played my cards right and reported to officer training school, I would have made it" However, Keller was dealt a losing hand, but he did get to be a general, at least he thought he was.

A day or so after seeing the photos, Keller visited a cathedral in St. Louise where be began screaming and singing for no reason, he said.

Then he drove to the base to take over his post, giving anti-terrorism exercises, over the radio, which were procedures to follow in case of a terrorism penetration at the base. He police commander got a call from the other officers who were working at the post saying Keller had "lost it" he said, and that he refused to leave. I thought I was a four-star general", Keller said. " I thought I had general's Huyser's job. I refused to leave my post because I thought we were at war and terrorists had invaded the base."

His police commander tried to talk some sense into him and get him to leave and go home with his Air Force wife, Captain Dorothy Keller, but it was to no avail. Keller had to be strapped to a stretcher and taken to the medical center, where he was labeled with manic psychosis, he said. According to Netritionals.com manic psychosis is when people "have seemingly boundless energy and are ceaselessly active and easily distracted. They may not want to rest or sleep for 24 hours or more. Mental activity is sharply accelerated, and delusions of grandeur, persecution or invincibility are not uncommon. Most people in this condition seem to be utterly elated for no apparent reason, but some become unreasonable irate and hostile They may even have hallucinations. Despite all this, people experiencing full-blown mania generally believe they are functioning at peak efficiency.

"The cause of this disorder is not well understood, but there are several theories as to its origin. It may be triggered by extreme stress. Heredity may be a factor in some cases. After the diagnosis with manic psychosis, Keller was cross-trained to be a member of the management engineering team at the base. However, he was medically boarded out of the Air Force in March 1981 after he began shouting to God at the National Prayer Breakfast a month before. "It was the end of a brilliant career," Keller said. Keller has been hospitalized on numerous occasions throughout the years after being discharged from the Air Force. He was last hospitalized 1995, but now has his disorder under control through his faith in the Roman Catholic Church and his doctor's orders, he said. It has taken him more than 12 years to write his book, which documents the journey he has had with manic psychosis, he said. He is currently finishing his third rewrite before his book will be published by iuniverse on the internet.. He moved to Sidney five years ago to be closer to his two sons, Daniel 24, and David, 17, who both live in Beavercreek, along with his ex-wife. "I absolutely love Sidney" , Keller said. "This is where I plan to live the rest of my life"

I just loved General "Dutch" Huyser because he treated me with kindness. He was a general's general   He loved freedom and he loved his troops. I am saddened with his passing away. This is a great loss to the Air Force. I loved him like a father. I wanted him to notice me. The day I got his framed signed picture, as well as General Ryan's, stands out. Dorothy's party cake as I was about to leave for Officer's Training School also has impact. Manic psychosis broke into my life Labor Day of 1980 and changed my world forever.

DISCHARGE SUMMARY

Dept of Veteran's Affairs
Roanoke, VA
Regional Office
02 Sept 1998

Disabled American Veterans

NAME OF VETERAN:
K.J.KELLER

ISSUE
Evaluation of bipolar disorder currently evaluated as 100%

EVIDENCE:
Hospital report from the Dayton VA Medical Center   Report
from Dr. Adityanjee dated 21 Apr 98

DECISION:
1. Evaluation of bipolar disorder, which is currently 100
   percent disabling, is continued.

REASONS AND BASES

1. The evaluation of bipolar disorder is continued as 100
   percent disabling is assigned whenever there is evidence
   of total occupational and social impairment, due to such
   symptoms as: gross impairment in thought processes or
   communication; persistent delusions or hallucinations,
   grossly inappropriate behavior; persistent danger of hurting
   self or others intermittent inability to perform activities of
   daily living (including maintenance of minimal personal
   hygiene); disorientation to time or place, memory loss for
   names of close relatives, own occupation , or own name.

The veteran was hospitalized on March 2 1998 after being found to be manic with religious, philosophical and theological preoccupation. He was distractible and had flight of ideas, pressured speech and euphoric mood. He was admitted to the high intensity psychiatric ward and his medications was adjusted. He was very cooperative but continued to be elated, euphoric, and with increase in psychomotor activity and manifesting numerous grandiose delusions. The veteran was persuaded to go to a group home and was discharged on March 17 1998. He was to follow up in Mental Health Clinic in 2 weeks.

In his report, Dr Adityanjee stated that the veteran was mentally impaired as he has increased in psychomotor activity, elation, and flight of ideas, pressured speech, jocular and playful behavior, and grandiose and persecutory delusions. He also exhibited poor insight and judgement. Dr Adityanjee stated that the veteran was not taking his medications and that he was making inappropriate decisions. Diagnosis of bipolar disorder was continued.

"open letter" for your information:

23 May 03
Sidney, OH 45365

Dear Dan and Dave,

At 52 you would think I would have some words of wisdom to pass on to my sons. I served my nation in the Air Force with honor, married to your mother. I have been mentally ill for years, while you were young, and needed a father. I've been in jail, for disturbing the peace, and lived on the streets of Dayton OH.

All I know is that my father was never there and I thought he hated me, so I hated myself. Self-Esteem is the best thing you can do to avoid manic-depression. I have been manic-free for five years in July 1. All I know is that I follow doctor's orders and avoid alcoholic drinks, and fast women. I do not have girlfriends, I have soul mates. Sex is not a part of my life. My belief system in the catholic faith has saved me from self-destroying my life.

Psychosis is pure hell on earth. Nothing is more terror, than to lose your mind. Manic frightens people. Manic is why I spent 92 days in jail for spilling coffee and yelling at the top of my lungs at the police. Manic is why I am divorced from your mom. Manic is why I have a daughter out of wedlock. Manic is why you never had a father when you were young. I don't care what you do in life as long as you never see manic-depression, or jail.

Now the best thing that ever happened too me was the day you were born. I was so happy that I had sons. Your mom was first to have me over to her mom's house for steak dinner. I was 17. She was the first REAL girlfriend I had ever had. Marylyn was just a flirt. The fact is I was spoiled. The fact is in 12 years your mom, never lied to me. I was totally unprepared for the head games of "Cris". Your mom was real. She never had time for games.

The fact is I was never there for your mom. I was a bad father, and a bad husband. I was bad with money. I spend money like water. I have lived in a dream world all my life. Normal was too boring to me. I have never been accused of being normal. The fact is while your mom was in the honor society I wanted to be a rock star. . I have always liked your mom. Even when she divorced me, I cried on the shoulder of "Cris". I knew I earned my divorce. One point I never cheated on your Mom with "Cris". She was walking wounded too from her divorce.

My brother Douglas is everything that I am not. He is a very successful person. I am not. I am not happy with my life. I am happy I had 12 years with your mom. I am happy I have two sons. Since I haven't seen my daughter since 1 year, I don't know what that is. My greatest joy is that my sons are normal. Your mother is the product of that one. If you hate your father, you will hate yourself. My father is 80 and feeling his age. He has worked hard all his life and his body is failing. Please be kind to your grandfather and write him and send cards. He at 80, is finally loving his wife and has stopped yelling at her. Mom broke her hip and he was her nurse. He let mom get a dog. He feeds the dog steak. Your grandfather is not going to live forever. He has heart problems and high blood sugar.

The most honest thing I can say about myself is that I am a fool but in another life I could have been a famous actor. I love drama, which is why I have 300 channels on my 52 inch TV. I write and for 12 yrs I have been working on my journal.

Veteran's House made sure took my meds for 5 years. All month I would look forward to seeing my sons. The source of my escape was Lee's Chinese and the Sidney movies.

Audrey was a good director and a very moral person. Yvonne my African-American , wife died last Oct of alcoholic addiction.

In closing all I can say is no father was ever more proud of his sons as I am. I think of you everyday and know you will do well because your mother has done a wonderful job. I hope your mom and I will be friends till Jesus.

27 May 03

"If you hate your father you will hate yourself. You hate your father because you think he hates you. The fact is he really doesn't hate you, he just doesn't have a clue how to deal with fatherhood."

Kevin John Paul Keller

A Shrink " Pearl ",of the Air Force psychiatric Hospital Malcolm Grow, Andrews AFB

"Your father loves you but can not give you what he doesn't have"

1981   March

"Self esteem begins each morning with Irish Spring and hot water. St. Pat was the first saint of the Irish, 400AD, and drove the snakes out of his country with a Callaway Driver #1, $500.00. "

Kevin John Paul Keller
JAN 2002

"Hate your father enough and you will hate your body and refuse to wash it with soap and hot water. Wash your body with soap and hot water. Kill your demon of self- hate…that wishes you the angel of death!!! "

Kevin John Paul Keller
JAN 2000

"The premise of our culture is the exploitation of the non-significant other, in order to feed the wants, needs, and desires, of self. At the expense of the non-significant other.

But self is but illusion...for the axe was laid to tree, in the Baptists time. The only sanity of reason is cross of Christ...all else is but sham...pretense... and glitter.

The toxic street water waste of greed, lust and power, shall be grace water washed in the light of goodness, kindness, and generosity, as the true cross of Christ.

Father your lost child has given up quest for chased mind mill...and now seeks affirmation of personhood. "

Kevin John Paul Keller

1993   JAN

VA MEDICAL CENTER
SALEM, VIRGINIA

"BLESSED ARE THE BROKEN HEARTED FOR THEY SHALL SEE GOD"

Father lost children are we... wandering lonely echoed 1935 white brick corridors... our worn torn dream sails tattered... blood spattered wide glass shattered...

Our heart soul wounds salt packed hard in basement corridors do these broken children play......

Father lost child am I...trying to find way back home to my fathers house that at 19 years I left in pained rejection..

Sentenced endless thereafter to seek the affirmation of chased mind mill...this conquistador.... Ready to follow home any dysfunctional soul……and is it not paradox those very lonely soul white bricked corridors……

Bespeak the very trappings of human spirit in further quest of chased mind mill , in the continuum of the hellish demons…

the dark night of soul………..

PSYCHOSIS

The only way to beat Disneyland is to face the pain…. and paint your lifescript with TRUE COBALT BLUE…….

FOR THE GLITTER PAINTS… ONLY DELAY RE-ENTRY…….

The wicked war games…over this little boy blue now come home to a clean white page…this fool who ran into blenders…following angels with tarnished wings…with hot tar words…….cold chilled the surgical steel heart…burning pained eyes tearing heart from lung… as if glass pained our blood spitted tattered salt wind torrents…

These little ones caught in rip tides our searing hot tar words so wounderous these wicked war games….we are but broken Eucharist….grace water flowing from wounds of the crucified Christ……….

This little boy come home to a clean white page…….

This pristine pastel……dawned the eschatological prophetic chrism………..

FROM AGE TO AGE INVADING MEN'S SOUL IN QUEST OF HER WISDOM

1993   Kevin John Paul Keller

Schizo – Affective

1994

She was chain smoking when I noticed her…something of her eyes…I think as we spoke…she was looking so lost and forgotten….Behind the chain linked fence…we lost no time finding her room…on the locked Salem Psych Ward. We hooked up after release and married in Virginia Beach VA in August of 1994. Actually the marriage had no chance because we were both lost to psychosis. She had brown deep eyes, as she chain smoked cigarette after cigarette. Downing one Budweiser after another, until she would pass out and start the process all over again.

She loved me I guess, but loved Budweiser more! After her multitude of releases from Salem VA Medical Center upon arriving at home the first thing she would do would be to flush all her meds down the toilet, and begin popping buds again The home trailer was cute. The audio stereo was awesome. It was expansive and at least $5,000. Her phone in her bedroom, was that of a pig. Which I always found interesting.

This pink pig was also found on fridge door. She would eat her "chitin's" . She would cook chitin's in the kitchen and stink up the trailer. Being a "white bread" Long Island Boy , I never knew of this southern dish.

I suppose you had to cultivate a taste for this dish! She had 6 bank accounts which totaled a grand total of $100,000.00. When I arrived from the psych ward that she had been just 2 weeks before and saw the bank accounts, knowing my girlfriend wanted to get married, I figured this was a grand proposition. She relayed to me that she would give up the booze if I married her, so in august of 1994 we got married in Virginia Beach.. $100,000.00, my God I had never seen that kind of money in my lifetime. Well, the first thing we did was buy a Honda Prelude for $24,000 dollars. Cherry red and very smooth and fast. Oh, I loved that machine. 1994 was my year for sure. After we traveled to Virginia Beach to get married, upon arriving at Virginia Beach we found the justice of the peace and his Native Indian motif office. The ceremony was brief and witnessed and my mouth salivated over the joint bank account that we would be setting up We had a 3 day honey moon in Virginia Beach before heading back to Danville VA.

At the motel my schizo -affective wife chain smoked salem cig's and consumed bud after bud. My wife had so many DUI'S on her driving record that she would never be legal on the road. The last wreck she totaled and was in the front yard. I became her chauffeur. I drove her all over this mostly black community. We created quite a show at her solid black church. Of course the first thing I did when the money was deposited was order "Callaway " golf clubs, $1,000 just for the irons. Of course I was slightly manic with that kind of money. I paid top dollar for my Callaway clubs. However, I did not bother asking my new wife's permission about this purchase. I wanted the clubs so I bought the clubs. Worst than that I sent my father $1,500 for his legal bills over my out of wed lock daughter Chrissie, from another relationship. When my new bride learned of these transactions she was enraged. She took her money out of joint savings and opened a savings account in her name only. So as usual my brief windfall was short-lived.

We joined the Danville Virginia Golf Course and paid for lessons. I showed up with my $1,000 golf clubs that I could not hit the ball with as I watched others with beat up clubs far excel my efforts. I immediately gained attention as the worst golfer on the course with the most expensive clubs. Most embarrassing was watching a 15 yr old hit the ball 300 yards as I couldn't get 150 yards straight. His old beaten clubs far exceeded mine. There came a time when my schizo- affective wife joined me on the golf course. She had a pretty golf outfit. Her job was to drive on the club grounds and not drink alcohol. She obeyed. She even valiantly struggled to learn the game of golf. Of course she was the only Afro-American on the course. But she did love driving me around on the golf cart. She did her duty well. She was a good wife. It is a shame that we didn't have a chance to make our marriage work due to our mental disorders.

We went on vacation for our second honeymoon, after Virginia Beach. We traveled to Myrtle Beach, South Carolina. We booked a progressive Hotel covered in lights. As soon as we unpacked my wife popped the bud. The room was non-smoking. Big mistake. She was smoking one Salem after another. It was a cold, and rainy day. My wife would not leave her room. The golf courses there were amazing. My wife was paying for all of this but all she wanted to do was pass out on bud. The Hotel was a work of art. It was there I bought my Indiana Jones cowboy hat. Finally I had enough of this drinking shit and booked the show at the Alabama Theater. The show was fab. My wife didn't drink. Thank God. Then I booked the show at the early 900 AD. jousting match. This was way cool. The horses and Knights and food was delightful… The steak and bread and soup came without fork or knife -- because they were not used in that time period.

Sad to say she finally passed away Oct 2002. I know not where she is buried. I miss her laugh and eyes. I miss her dark skin. When she got psychotic I just took off before the cops would arrive for some violation of current law. This is sad. We never had a chance to make our marriage work. We both were mentally ill and that's not good for a marriage. I wasn't a good husband because you don't marry someone for their money but I did.

SGT KEVIN JOHN KELLER USAF (RET.)

3 May 2003

Sidney, OH 45365

Open letter

Dear Dot

This is to affirm the delight of seeing my sons Easter Sunday. I realize you had a lot to do with allowing this brunch to happen.

I live with the awareness I wasn't a good father, when my sons were little. I miss my sons and I was wondering if you could remind the boys to call Sundays

One more thing that bothers me. Years ago it was said I cheated on you. I never cheated on my son's mom. Please let my sons know the truth. I admit I was a jerk and a flirt.

GOD BLESS

29 May 2003
Sidney, OH 45365

Dear Dan and Dave

Self Esteem kills manic psychosis. I drove myself to the dark night of soul: psychosis.

"Cris" and I were going thru divorce from our spouses at the same time. The pain of divorce from our spouses destroyed our emotional balance, and friendship.

BOOK TWO

PRELUDE

———————— Chapter One ————————

1989 Feb

Virginia Beach VA

It's…hot…water…now…water…hot   running….nachos… and parked car kisses…. foggy windows… eyes so vivid… so burning….

"Oh Kevin…you're just going to find another woman.. and forget all about me…she'll be intuitive…like me… probably called Molly"

I should have known…here it comes… the ice…god…I hate the ice water…why is this women a kitchen faucet.. of ice or scalding water?????????

"same old Kevin… the emotions of a 7 year old…loud… abrasive and controlling…. I don't want to go out with you Kevin…I really like Jim a lot… I don't like you Kevin…I really am not interested in you…you're not my type…I only called back in Jan…for the money… I'm heavily dating Jim"

"so Cris… only nice to Kevin ..until the bills paid,… right Cris……?"

"Right!!!!!!!"

1989 Oct

It's running warm……..she's pastels of simplicity…… eyes full of texture…. I carrying pumpkin……full of milky way bars……she carrying eyes of expression saying quite profoundly…….God, Kevin I'm so very sorry…

"God bless you Cris…"
"God bless you Kevin"

He now turning towards street…. mounting trusty steel steed
…voice now calling out….

"Kevin. this card…its from your mom. you sent it to me…
please take it…."

"God…look at those eyes. where does she get those eyes.?

Feel the heat?..feel the energy…..God they're on fire….
Where does she get those eyes??????

The night air……it's always so talking at night…it's colors…..
flood the mind. and voices of emotion with pastels

MID- OCT 1989

The waters still running warmer…her eyes dancing in delightful
and charming colors..seagulls.thrilled as one approached…
landing next to us……

"Oh Kevin look he's talking to us.."
"So "Cris", ..what happened to Marty?"

"I'm not talking about it Kevin…if only you'd be more
consistent like this…it would be fine Kevin.."

I kissed her twice. I'm sorry but I couldn't help it. I'm totally
captivated by her…

"Cris don't you age.."

"Oh yes. Kevin"

"Where?"

"Look around my eyes. see? that's why I wear glasses, see?"

Take your glasses off Cris", she did.

"Cris you're fine wine...just fine wine!"

I keep telling you...she's a kitchen faucet.. the girl's hot or cold running water...God...when she's running hot... ...look out... grab hold... of your socks.. and better get ready for the after burners.......better strap yourself in...

When she's cold better have portable heater...lots of kerosine.. it's a long winter with this one...this fawn is scared to death of what her heart feels...here she is. cute very cute...it's dark car night... late she so very tired...her buns cute in tight jeans...

There's her ex.. barking inside trailer...I looking for a nearby muzzle...he's a fear biter and I don't have rabies vaccine.

"Kevin. I'm tried of being pursued. I just want you as friend I'm not seeing anyone and neither should you. I need to get closer to God. how would you feel if I married someone else? I need someone stable and someone consistent. Why can't you be like Nathan. You're a computer. You want me to go out with you. You want me to kiss you. You want me to love you. You want me to marry you. Kevin it's very flattering to get flowers but I don't love you. I don't want you to love me"

IT'S MID NOV 1989 RUNNING COLD

"Kevin I do avoid you. I don't want to spend a lot of time with you."

This is great, I buy her children a birthday cake, yet she can't find the time to share it with me. Never a birthday card. Never a birthday gift. Never even a thank you card for me. God it's cold mid nov. I pass flowers to her, at stopped car, before the light changes green. Still no time of day for Kevin. He's just leftovers. She looking for men of interest. Men of romance. Steak dinner as I scrub pans in cooks kitchen. I'm peeling potatoes. Occasionally filling her empty wine glass. Foggy window shut.

I find self sitting with long time friend.

"Kevin love is not a victim of your emotions but a servant of your will. Are you strong enough to accept only what she can give, right now? God, Kevin when are you going to take the hint?

It's warm chapel cozy. I talking just back from New York. Good feeling about me. So good feeling. Maybe things are just going to come around. Here she comes passing behind me. She smiling that amazing smile. Bright eyes god I feel the heat. She's now blushing with embarrassment.

"Kevin but you don't know all the details because they are important. You will know why it's over with Marty."

Marty how long will I have to put up with this boy? This boy who delights in game playing. This is just delightful. I'm paying the bills playing provider for a dysfunctional family. I'm a court jester not even asking sex. A broken hearted fool, trying somehow to cope with the loss of my family. Court jester am I lost in pain. Running from a cave-in. Hard now trying not to know what is so hard to accept . My blindness cost me my most precious gems

DEC 1989

God I feel bad. I gave away my son's video tape. It was his favorite tape. I didn't even know it. God I feel bad. I keep asking Cris for it back. She could care less. I'm just leftovers. I get called only when she needs more bills paid. It's so horridly cold.

So in my pained manhood now crushed, I find myself now a cold, cold hearts whipping boy. Here you are boy, fido good dog meat. Catch here's some more pain. Does it taste good? I have you almost trained now. Can you jump higher? Miss your sons, good , you can't see my kids either. You're just leftovers to us.

God it's cold in this winter's frost. My male ego frostbitten. This is just lovely. Lord have you a portable heater you could loan me until spring?

To be appreciated, I mean isn't that really it? Isn't that what you're really after? I mean it's really simple. You want to know you're of value in her eyes. So here you are, paying the bills, fending off the wolves, at the front door, clubbing to death the piranha in the fish tank. You wish she would affirm your manhood. I mean to have you're girl come to you as you're flexing muscle, over shark-infested waters, she cooing in the background, "what a big strong man you are, are you James Dean incarnate?

BUT WHAT HAPPENS...RIGHT....YOU'RE WOODY ALLEN GETTING SERVED GLASS GROUNDS IN MORNING COFFEE. She now can get on with men of interest, someone in style.

It's a one way street sucker. It's this cobra who wants blood and you're a nazi yelling at her at the top of your lungs. Smart move sucker.

WAIT A MINUTE...BUT MY NAZI YELLING AND MY BOA CRUSHING HER SPACE...WERE IN SELF DEFENSE. IT WAS MY PAIN TALKING.

So what sucker. You lose big time on this deal...she gets her car fixed as you hock your computer system.

HIT THE ROAD...WHAT DO YOU WANT FLOWERS??

Go cry in church pew...fool.

But you don't understand silver fox, I really wanted to be her spider killer, to flex muscle over shark-infested waters, and have those amazing chestnut eyes that stun me to stillness as if smooth stone skipped, off mirrored pond, look up at me, telling me in wordless novel chapters….

YOU'RE GREAT

TEACH ME STILLNESS SILVER FOX…..

Oh silver fox what I wouldn't do for a "gee whiz" I think you're great letter. I mean just to know that perhaps, I'm not really a woody allen to her. Perhaps a simple hug.

Oh silver fox just something sweet and simple. I was man enough to pay bills yet not man enough for her to go out with???????????????

NEW YEAR'S EVE 1990

Here sitting am I at Paul's, such peace here, such gracious couple. God what have I done?????????

"of course Kevin she's afraid….wouldn't you be???

She really is afraid, she's seen you really weird.

Entering trailer in mid of night"

GOD WHEN CHERYL SAYS THINGS LIKE THIS, DO I SEE HOW STUPID I CAN BE

DEC 1986

Kevin is at Dorothy's door. He finds himself locked out.

All locks changed on his town house. He's pacing…driving all night. Driving all night. Where to go?????????

What to do?????????/ my life shattered.. a cave-in…no where to go. It's just him, his clothes, and few bucks in wallet. Finally exhaustion hits…as car finds itself heading towards "Cris'", the port of peace. Horrid the night I lost family, the night of lock out.

Sitting am I now……. It's night light moon full…silence now deafening screaming at me to be still fool. Be still

1967

Arthur killed Wendy. He floated her tied to raft, as the clipping in "NEWSDAY", .said. The event blew my mind.

They reported her hands and feet tied to raft. The south bay of Long Island. Her hair matted and tangled in lobster pot,

floating the south bay of Long Island New York……………

SO LOOKING TOWARDS YOU SILVER FOX I TOLD WENDY'S MOM

"Wendy's a living part of all of us… of all her touched for she's life's continuum, impacting upon all elements, for as one element impacts element all are interconnected the bio-mass integration, the final resolution."

"as I spill water from cup to ground, the ground feeds dirt, the dirt feeds flower, the flower, feeds steer, the steer feeds man"

"we give birth to each other's self, in the very air we breathe, we breathe Wendy's air."

"Yes, silver fox, you taught me this. You taught me that all negatives must be translated in positives, for all energy is resident, in but different form"

"Fuel my heart's furnace silver fox, to burn with love for innocence lost, now found, anew. Let me serve this innocence and build castle to the sky, of where heaven and earth kiss holy hand"

VALENTINE'S DAY 1990

It's new waves, the seagulls calling, as I sit amidst the seagulls flying around , so cool. The gulls , they would be flying around "holy family" school playground, back in 1964. What happened silver fox to Kevin the altar boy??????

This boy the nuns taped his mouth shut?????????
Dorothy tree climbing friend since 4th grade, filled hallways with laughter.

What happened silver fox, to that boy that loved to church sit for hours, looking at the huge cross on altar, in empty church.

What happened, thinking, pondering, looking introspectively at self, simple values, noble ways, objective truth.

Absolutes of Faith, and simple paths to Jesus.

Hours looking at a hug gold cross, still there in hallway first graduation class of "holy family" 1964. Kevin always the loner, always out of place.

I spent my growing years living inside my head, and when lonely, singing classic in stilled air.

The pain games of others hurt me profoundly, berating me. Silver fox you knew all along why, no one feels comfortable with the odd, the different, the out of place.

They laughed the class clown: Thomas Aquinas. It's seagulls... flying... thank you silver fox...in their talking I hear you. Why do you send seagulls to talk to me?????

I now, lost in the calls of the gulls, feeling the dry air chill, like grandfather's, in Baldwin, New York, Long Island. The pond, frozen, and I skating, grandmother busing kitchen, to the feeding, as china settings stood in troop cadence, lined officers, ready for inspection.

Dorothy now my ex, she understood , me, we climbing trees at Bayard arboretum, among white goose, vast green lawn, islands of rare flowers, and curved nature walks, of stone, composing classics upon classic guitar, writing prose, among cedar trees. We climbing trees, talking the ways of world and classics, wondering how to end unjust war in the Asian jungles.

The night of the memorial at Salisbury park to end the unjust war the hills alive with lit candle and night burning floods of poets and playwrights back from the village, burning candles in rain.

Remember silver fox.... The planting fields and Frisbee tossing... the fun of 1968...enjoy the flowers, me driving cab, paying way for dot, to graduate, the ice storms nights of SUNY Binghamton, my creative friends, and the printing of "Dune".

Moved SUNY to escape the quicksand of Robin.... She found a fool...lost in clouds.... For her spider killer, lost in Never Never Land, not seeing the piranha in the pond.

It was my tree climbing friend since 4th grade that rescued me from Robin, the truth of her words broke through the clouds of delusion and deceit and yet marriage to Dot was not my cure, for still burning was the rage I carried for my father. Oh, silver fox, to find bread from ovens and blue berry pie, and that rare roast beef, god, where did grandma find those wonders????????????

Hours lost to grandpa's basement of books, tapes, and films. Silver Fox can I revisit those lost hours of fun????

SGT KEVIN JOHN KELLER USAF (RET.)

LOVE IS THE EXPANSION OF ONE'S OWN OR ANOTHER'S SPIRITUAL GROWTH…
TRANSLATING THE COMMON BREAD OF SELFHOOD, INTO THE TRANSLUCIDITY OF LIVING MANNA

You sly fox whose revelations have transformed burning candle of heart, into blinding introspection, your countenance, flooding my room into sea of light

THERE IS ONLY ONE WAY TO BEAT DISNEYLAND, YOU MUST FACE THE PAIN AND PAINT YOUR LIFESCRIPT, ONLY WITH TRUE COBALT BLUE, FOR THE GLITTER PAINTS ONLY DELAY-RE Entry

TRANSITION:

———— CHAPTER TWO ————

92 Day Isolation at a jail in Virginia for contempt of court by sending flowers to "Cris" after a judge ordered no contact and during that stay going manic as an inmate of the jail thus placed on "Medical Hold"

OCT 1991

":Blood" was my stickman in the "puzzle palace"
he cost me a carton of Newport… I used name "eagle" as I was sent… from tank 2 to the "birdcage". I was glad to get away from "Eddie"… Eddie was the houseman of tank 2. And was really pissed off that the turnkeys were stupid enough to place the "cracker" on his turf…

"Blood" got me extra hot dogs stolen from the kitchen crew for a extra pack of Newport…. He liked the cracker singing psalms from this catholic prayer book. I did this to stay sane in City Jail. As I would scream for the shrink that never showed. 60 days now in isolation of section one… as the gays had a food fight with their fecal matter with urine squirted from plastic container

This cracker finding himself in the bammer cells of section one under "protective custody"…wandering deeper into the evergreen Forest flooring of Disneyland. The stainless steel toilet now was my laboratory to wash my hands for now I envisioned…myself as DR Martin Luther King. screaming thru echoed wasteland of section one "Dr Martin Luther King was a prophet of god"….drinking now my own urine.

The viper of psychosis progressively street water washing my once pure catholic bread thoughts of 13, to the toxic wasteland of lust…rage… and slow burning mindscape of planned revenge…. Against…the vixen who put me here. Instead of having a classic manic depressive hospitalized for treatment as she hit my bank account for 5k…knowing the fool couldn't do a thing to prevent this…..

"stickman…can you place a call through the pipeline to Laura?"

"no problem"

"1 pack of Newport…ok?"

"sure"

Laura true friend for 10 yrs and not one lie yet…my bammer cell a montage decorum of national geographic medium.. the background earth tones and survival instinct of the animal kingdom displayed the artistic spirit of the bammer cells previous occupant.

The roaches… and silverfish came free of charge… and served to remind me things could be worst.. I was off the streets…to the cutting edge were the pictures of police brutality on cell block hallway…facing the bammer cell as if silent reminder to the turnkey

To the bammer cell on the left was "juicy" and to the bammer cell on the right was "new York"… my next court date was 4 nov and the moment I hit section one "juicy" delighted in playing my nemesis… as if intuitively realizing sleep deviation would enhance my manic episodes…

The constant banter of the she/he demon was maddening… I sought refuge in writing prose to the vixen that placed me here in my addiction to emotional abuse and torrent of manic psychosis.

In my manic state of mind, this of course is common sense, when a judge orders you to stop sending flowers stop writing stop apologizing and calling the significant other of your life…………

It is perfectly acceptable behavior to martyr yourself to life in section one bammer cell sharping pencil on concrete floor, to send more letters, so you can receive more pain, we like pain, because true love always bleeds, nothing twisted here.

We trade off one obsessive compulsive addiction for another, envisioning myself Dr Martin Luther King, the visionary of civil rights, granted me the illusion of a suffering saint. Father of civic rights, imprisoned for the truth, of his words, thus I start singing with all my manic energy, through the echoed section one bammer cells , the national anthem .

"hey cracker…I told you to cut that shit out…."

This mop handle comes flying through bars….

It's the hall man…built like bull elephant

I'm too manic to realize how close I'm coming to real pain. Physical pain…. I love the guy… don't know why….

I love his simplicity not all concerned for the power of pain the guy can unleash upon me

"now listen homeboy,,,I don't want to hurt you cracker…but if you don't cut the crap I'm gonna hurt you bad!!!!!!!!!!"

"Blood " my stickman is bringing me donuts..he's telling me to shut up before I start to bleed.

"hey Blood, why are you wearing a white cross. You're black muslim…????????????"

"I know but I know you're not… and I know you're scared!!!"

OUT OF JAIL

4 May 1992

so much pain…the rain darkened streets we wander…
as the lion…roams seeking whom he can devour. back up you've passed the green light… as you now are offering your heart to a blender. an angel with tarnished wings.

28 May 1992

saw the boys last sat…… we played at the lake at the Dayton VA Medical Center. The boys hugged me as they jumped from the wall. It was beautiful..to be hugged by them.

EASTER HERE WAS THE MOST ALIENATED DAY OF MY LIFE AS I SAT IN EMPTY AUDITORIUM WATCHING OLD BLACK AND WHITE FILMS OUT OF FOCUS.

5 Dec 1992

My conversation with Dot was again one sided……I am reduced to fatherhood through cards and letters…occasional visits…she has held my last letters because they were too emotionally heavy

it was labor day weekend…1980 with plastic fork in hand as I watched across from me a man trying to find his face.. to feed himself.

Psychotic... as I was fearing to again see those red blood marks of the viper on the wall. It drained my power to fend off CIA operatives in surveillance… then I was brought into room of white robed professionals. My thorazine trance turned to terror as I opened my mouth to speak. yet only found my body twisting involuntary and unable to speak.

Wasn't it just days before this alienated and lowly Sgt was ready to ship off to Officer's Candidate School.   After 29 credits and degree complete achieving outstanding military honor serving under Gen Huyser:...Commander in Chief: Military Airlift Command…serving national resource, As Elite Guard Troop. Yet, now the only image to be imprinted through barred windows were the hamburgers grilling labor day weekend below on picnic bench., as families united.

Now, having proven for sure my sickness to a room full of white robed professionals…,my veins, full of chemicals…I fell to my knees and prayed with silent despair…"Lord. get me out of here"

Then , suddenly as manna from heaven…weeks passed and melted to days… as Dorothy appeared with Goldernberg's Chocolate Candy Bars

BEST DAMN Chocolate Bar Ever….

She said we were going home. She was my rock of stability. She was best friend since tree climbing 4 th grade.

I hadn't seen her since she was crying at the 375th security police squadron.. hearing me shouting for someone to send me a Christian to pray with .after I had just pulled off yet another military exercise and totally lost it.

WHY THE HELL HADN'T ANYONE TOLD ME THAT RICKY HAD JUST BEEN DUMPED BY HIS GIRLFRIEND WHEN I TORE INTO HIM FOR SCREWING UP AN

EXERCISE AND HUMILIATED HIM IN FRONT OF THE FLIGHT????

Did I know he was going to just hours later drive his car into a tractor trailer?????????????????????????????????

Don't you see silver fox, all my life I wanted to be someone, famous, as if the final act would compensate for the neglect of my father..........and endless words of disaffirmation tearing down self esteem

I was 19 when I left my father's rage. Get treated like dirt and you begin to think you're dirt. I was 30 when I stood up to him. I told him what he was, a nasty son of a bitch.

Yet his catholic wife would take his rage. Catholics seem to relish pain as a saintly act

That's why we believe Priests can live on air. And Sisters can always be found to carry our load. We have created our own slave trade, and pass it off as godliness.

This catholic school bred boy was only to find further alienation and emotional pain in class as he over-compensated to gain attention and affirmation and inclusion, and only claim to fame was to gain the highest class average for getting slapped the most by sister !!!!!!!!!!!!!!!!!!1

It was never my idea to leave home in the first place, with "Sean" in 1969. The idea was his. What I didn't know was that once tasting the street at 19 with $92.00 to my name. this white bread boy was to be conditioned to continue a destructive cycle that would last 2 decades.

He also broke his mother's heart. The one person whose love and faith he adopted as his own. While his father who really couldn't give a damn in the first place…now had more kindling for the fire.

Silver Fox…don't you see…I now had the attention of the command staff….and now this amazing labor day weekend shame overwhelmed me…as I approached the 375th security police squadron the guys were trying to give "crazy cop" a second chance. Yet we all knew the dream of gold bars on my shoulder was over. So I found myself waxing The Police Commander's car…he laughed at his own disability .shortness and asked me where the blocks were for his brake and accelerator pedals.

I was enraged when my sterling record was now tarnished with "borderline psychosis". I suppose the shrink thought it cute to mention in discussion "god is good isn't she"

All my efforts to keep him from entering those words were in vein. His closing remarks were "when you're pregnant.. you're pregnant."

My medication to this new word "psychosis" was Jesus. My silent prayer was "God first. Listen to the wise words of my wife…. And repeat step one…God first"

What of the wise words of my wife, how was it I failed to notice what my emotional peaks and lows were putting her through, how hard she was trying to support me

I was working day and night. Never seeing the kids. Working as a cop during the day and as a student at night.

At the stars and bars banquet she brought me a $400 suit, $400 class ring, $100 brief case. $200 London top coat.

She so proud…she threw a party for me before I was to leave for Officer's Training School….my mind still embracing the cake.

Those days I could jog the 7 mile flight line…as my body and spirit would experience a spiritual cleansing at 4 miles….

The command was truly trying to help. I was being cross trained to the management engineering team because of the industrial technology degree.

I broke again from reality at the National Prayer Breakfast, the delusional state of a manic episode overwhelming me.. now ending a career in blue for sure…strapped down once again being air-evaced to Malcolm Grove Medical Center Andrews AFB. My veins filled once again with thorazine…. Dot's eyes were in agony as we met up with one another, just moments before the flight

At Malcolm Grow med center Dr Pearl Leona said

"YOUR FATHER LOVES YOU BUT CAN NOT GIVE YOU WHAT HE DOESN'T HAVE"

It was during an intense psychotherapeutic session that I cried out alarming all there….. and when asked later to explain, I made the statement, that came from nowhere, "WHEN THE DAM BURSTS IT DOESN'T ASK THE VALLEY IF IT'S READY"

You see silver fox, when you bury emotions alive they come back in twisted form, years of pain, were now cascading over the dam, I had now found my quest and when my parents came to visit, I hugged my dad, and told him. I loved him. I then announced I now wished to be a saint.

Helen my mother and a very good catholic went to her priest in Hicksville, New York and cried out "my son's writing religious poetry and wants to be a saint and they have him locked up".

"Helen, god works in strange ways and honestly speaking some of the saints were peculiar" said the priest of my mother.

Loneliness and alienation gripping me, I would chant the psalms in echoed bathroom with all the manic energy I had

I FEARED LOSING DOROTHY WHICH DID I YEARS LATER

I realize now only too late I should have listened to the two enlisted troops visiting us back at Wright-Patterson…trying to warn me about enlistment in the cop field.

Silver Fox I had to prove myself. And when I saw that video tape of the USAF Elite Guard I was hooked. Look at those neat weapons rapelling of roof tops and shooting all the bad guys.

I had to take the hard road to 2nd LT through the enlisted ranks. I disregarded the ease of ROTC.

THE ONLY THING I DO REMEMBER OF THE DETECTIVES INTERVIEWING ME BACK IN 1960 WERE THOSE .38 SPECIALS. THIS AFTER SOME JERK KIDNAPPED ME WITH A $5.00 OFFER TO SHOVEL HIS SNOW ON HIS DRIVEWAY. I WAS A VERY YOUNG SCHOOL BOY WHOM THE NUNS NEVER PREPARED FOR THIS KIND OF SEX EVENT. WHEN HE UNZIPPED HIS PANTS I DOVE OUT THE DOOR INTO THE SNOW AT ABOUT 25 MPH. AT 28, I WOULD BECOME AN EXPERT MARKSMAN. MY MIND FEEDING EMOTION THAT NO ONE WOULD EVER HURT ME OR MY LOVED ONE. I WAS CHOSEN TO PROTECT NATIONAL RESOURCE. I GREW TO LIKE THE FEEL OF BLACK OILED GUN STEEL AND THE POWER BEHIND IT. SINCE 1981 AND MY PSYCHOTIC BREAK INTO MANIC EPISODE I HAVE NOT TOUCHED ONE

The mind is a strange animal isn't it SILVER FOX. ??

The macho power I had hoped to gain. Only served to unravel me, much like the loneliness and alienation of 1969 when

"Sean" stranded me in Peoria with $1.29 in our joint bank account. He cleaned me out and left town and I was left with YMCA rent due.

I worked a cardboard factory going through the emotional hunger of a 19 yr old alienated from parents and longing for his wayward girlfriend back home.

It was 1970 when "Sean" invited me to a camping trip at Wildwood State Park. Days later Wendy's body was found tried to raft hands and ankles bound, her long beautiful hair caught in lobster pots. "Sean" was never found.

Perhaps Silver Fox this explains the obsession for power and control, cold day in hell that someone would do that to me, there I was silver fox, rubbing elbows with generals, gaining their affirmation, after years of work, and then this, a locked psychiatric ward.

Emotional stability was never something I seemed to lay hold of very long after leaving home with "Sean" at 19. After Wendy's death, and "Sean" s disappearance, as Dot left for college in 1969, I allowed myself to get picked up at a party.

The word co-dependence was not coined in 1969. Robin introduced to sex in the basement of my grandmother's house. I was scared of this act that would condemn me to hell. It involved my penis, that reminded me of that locked car and pubic hair touch offer of $5.00 when I was kidnapped and escaped from the car of this madman.

Soon afterwards Robin would convince me the child she was carrying was mine. (joke, no way). We left New York and headed for Peoria. I worked the iron foundry. The dirt and sweat caked blue jeans, they were my red badge of courage. The men at the foundry found this trusting 19 yrs catholic bred boy they called New York a blast.

Silver Fox, I'm ashamed that I fell every time for their sucker jokes, and now at 52 speaking real , a pretty face and soft voice can still steal me blind

I've seem to become addicted to life on the edge. Those early 1970's were to build a foundation of emotional turmoil that I seem to yearn for.

Robin was soon on the phone with her well financed parents. I now was back on Long Island driving a truck for Orange Front paint store.

Robins's brother got into local 1298 construction. I'm sorry but the nuns failed miserably to prepare me for this. The jackhammers weighed more that I did, as I was easy prey. The family bought the lie we were married out in Peoria. The child was named "Faith Ann"

The cycles of co-dependency were only intensifying. I also learned the child was not mine.

April 1974 , I moved upstate to SUNY Binghamton. Poor as Dot and I were, 1974 to 1978 were best years of my life.

It was a fast-talking Air Force recruiter that talked us both into the Air Force. In the obsession for career, position and status, I sold my soul.

My power and energy totally engrossed now in the obsession of a hard degree, and the politics of the Air Force power struggle.

You know what I'm talking about Silver Fox, those early years, when we were so poor we walked to market for a ¼ pound of hamburger. We ran out of gas coming home from Chinese and laughing pushed the car home , throwing snowballs at the gold dome of the Greek Orthodox church, running in panic at the echo.

The day before I was to ship out, Dot threw me a party.

I NEVER ASKED HER ADVICE.

It was the biggest mistake of my life. It would never be the same after police combat training and indoctrination. Gaining machohood through assault team traing and weaponry is very stupid.

MANHOOD TO ME IS THIS, HAVING THE COURAGE TO PICK UP THE PIECES OF YOUR DYSFUNCTIONAL LIFE AND CREATE ART FOR ART'S SAKE

I now see the truth of those simple picnics, and celebrating fall with hot apple cider and donuts, writing love letters, yet at the time, these little things paled in comparison to gaining stature and career position.

Depression soon followed after being boarded out on a medical, my thorazine trance, now refined to mellarill, and haldol. To deaden my pain I saved soul via phone lines at the Christian Broadcasting Network, the 700 club. I found some truly good people at the 700 club.

I formed Keller Associates Ltd Jun 1986 and published the Tax Tutor and was first to market this tutorial for the CPA's.

I realized a 53% profit.

DEC 1986 WAS THE LOCK OUT AT CHRISTMAS LOCKED OUT OF MY OWN HOUSE, TOTALLY CAUGHT OFF GUARD, TO THIS UPCOMING DEVASTATION, THE FOOL SO LOST IN THOUGHT, AS NOT TO SEE, HIS OWN VULNERABILITY AND UPCOMING DESTRUCTION.

Silver Fox, giving it some thought perhaps this fool, finds himself inwardly, not deserving of the pleasures of stability and peace others take for granted. Perhaps I would plot to steal from myself, that which he finds he is not worthy of, his self esteem robbed of its own reward.

This is life on the edge, his constant struggle as proving ground, his silent contemplative prayer

"LORD SAVE ME FROM MYSELF"

RESOLUTION

—————— CHAPTER THREE ——————

In July 1998 to Jan 2003 I resided at Veteran's House in Sidney OH…This group home under the direction of Audrey, " saved" my tormented soul.

AUGUST 1999

"Father, I have seen your peace as my soul settles at Veteran's House. I accept my fate…my loss…is but yesterday year. Father we live as one- the family event was fabulous."

18 AUGUST 1999

"Father my money is gone. For 2 weeks my mind is whole.

19 AUGUST 1999

"Father your presence is here…as I sit waiting my time.

20 AUGUST 1999

Today I showered and dressed white shirt and tie.

Fishing found me 2 blue gill…talking with Ron. My father ,Arthur , called to tell me how proud he was…it was a great moment.

17 SEPT 1999

Praise God I don't owe $5,500. Writing, "Father", is a good idea. I'm waiting for Audrey…my mouth shot with nova cane.

Sunday September

I saw Dot and the Kids yesterday. We had Chinese food at Lee's Chinese. It was wonderful. David was scared by a spider. I've settled down to Sidney…no more psych wards.

27 Sept 1999

I have no pictures of David growing up. They are grown up now. I must accept the times.

3 Oct 1999

I have to have a life rooted in staying well like I have had this year and one and one half.

Oct 2000

Sent 2 dozen red roses to Dot. A cold is kicking my ass. Dad is writing me and so is Dot. My sons are calling on Sunday.

Spent 2 weeks in nursing home because Audrey was on vacation. Dot came with the boys. We ate Italian. I had " blackened" prime rib.

4 March 2001

Played golf Saturday. Saw sons today. Dot was nice. Not a golf day . Too cold. A day to read.

8 March 2001

Dan called. It was good. He and friend rented a house. I brought my "Callaway Hawkeye" $1,000 irons.

13 March 2001

Had all you can eat steak. Saw the movie "See Spot Run". Enjoying new shoes.

14 March 2002

Crushed golf ball…200 yards. Center fairway. 3 wood Hawkeye Callaway. Knocked the hell out of my 5 wood. Saw Lawyer. May is the month.

15 Nov 2005

It's David's birthday…we had a great time at Ponderosa…the steak was delightful…
Just got off the phone with Belona in Cebu city Philippines… she's so cute…Cebu girls are delightful…so pure and simple…I love her laugh…the kids are a joy

"Shelia" came over demanding $500. She was so upset the police were called.
Well I caved in and gave her $600. In Dec she'll get $400 and I'm done with her.

I'm sleeping well. This is very good. The boys returned computer on Sunday.
No audio on D:\ Drive. The system is old and has bugs.

21 Nov 05

Solar Systems got me audio…coming for music video pop up block

23 Nov 05

Solar Systems coming today…can't run videos…slow …

Why do I give my money away to girls???

You can't buy love…when I am going to learn this???
I'm always lonely…
So what… deal with it…
It just seems that ever since my divorce I've been trying to buy love
So what… deal with it
I have to get out of debt
I can't give money away!!!
Theresa is an angel…she won't take a dime from me because of my debt

Just saw Solar Systems…my unit only has 150 mega it's too old for 2005 videos
Not enough resource…this I understand…but what is a megahertz???

The unit will only support internet radio and CDs imported to the library
If I don't just leave this alone…I'm going to crash the system

24 Nov 05

Reflections of losing my daughter

All I remember is jail…taken to the judge…he then saying to me what am I going to do about my daughter….I then saying I'm bi-polar

when I am going to stand up to bi-polar????

Today Theresa and I are having a little Thanksgiving dinner. I'm not sending money to Roseanne…I'm not going to be used.

My first priority is to Dan and Dave. My sons come first. They are family. Why am I always chasing girls? When do I grow up??

Growing up means not overspending money…I just can't afford to send money to the Philippines…I don't even know Roseanne.

Belona I've known almost 2 yrs. I love her kids.

Just what is the problem with girls? Why am I never happy with the girl I've got?

25 Nov 05

Theresa prepared outstanding Thanksgiving dinner yesterday… It was a simple day…today saw cam of Belona Philippines…

She was such a doll…so very cute…in her sexy outfit…smiling at the cam…

My 150-megahertz system is a pain in the neck…can't wait for Solar Systems to replace it…

Maybe sometime in my lifetime I will heal of divorce…that would be nice!!!

29 Nov 05

I am haunted with my late wife Yvonne. How do I get over a dead wife?? I miss her and miss my ex-wife Dorothy. Theresa and I had romantic evening. I am haunted. I have lots of new friends on internet in Philippines. Theresa is up now so I will chat with her. My debt is getting better but I promise friends money on the Internet. This is stupid. How will I ever get out of debt that way? When do I heal??

When do I get over an ex-wife and a late wife??

30 Nov 05

I want to replace Dorothy and Yvonne. I want a wife. I'm

very lonely…and haunted. My debt is getting better and I'm sleeping now. I am slowly getting better but it takes time. Yvonne was such a sad girl. We really didn't have a chance. We met on a psych ward. She got out first and I came for a visit. I found out she had $100,000 in the bank so when she wanted marriage I said ok. The whole thing was dysfunctional from the start. She deserved better than the treatment she got from me. I wanted her money. Her love of drink ruined our marriage and of course there was the pot thing. I didn't know she was gay. She died with $80,000 in checking. It was sad. She wanted love. I gave pain. How do you compete with Budweiser? The home trailer was cute. She had her bedroom and I had mine. Not a day goes by I don't miss Yvonne or Dorothy. The truth is Dorothy murdered my heart and I took it out on Yvonne. This Christmas is a special time with Theresa. I try to be good friend. Last year I was on a psych ward. I'm trying to avoid that this year.

1 Dec 05

Just got a $946 phone bill because of the Philippines. This is stupid. Theresa deserves a better boyfriend. I call the Philippines instead of loving Theresa

And she has been good to me. I gave Theresa my money because she will guard it from me. I can't be trusted with money. Theresa is so good to me. She wants husband material. I can do better for her. She gave me a delightful Thanksgiving dinner. All I do is flirt with other girls. What's up with that. I must treat Theresa as a girlfriend and stop flirting with cyber friends in the Philippines. I blow money. I flirt. When do I treat Theresa right? She is so good. I'm going to chat with her now.

5 Dec 05

Paid off "Shelia" and got my stuff. As I look at photo album I reflect. The wedding photos are delightful…what happened? The lock-out Dec 86 crushed me. Many broken years followed. Last year I was in a psych ward again. I am stable now. I miss Dorothy but that's life. I must do better with Theresa. My divorce scares me of commitment. I play games. I lie. This year I will not lie or play games. Last year I chased Audrey and she wasn't interested in a boyfriend. This year I have Dot's spice rack. I must grow from my divorce. I must accept my past and move on. I just wouldn't leave "Cris" alone. My spice rack is of Dorothy.. The divorce is over. I must move on. My heart still is in love with Dot. We had history. Today Theresa wants a boyfriend. She has been kind and loving. My heart is afraid of love. "Cris" didn't love me and I did 92 days in jail over spilled coffee and flowers. Theresa isn't about that. She wants love. Life moves on. I must trust Theresa because she is worthy of love. Love is the expansion of one's own or another's spiritual growth. Why do I give Theresa a hard time. I don't trust love. I play games. When the divorce hit I ran to "Cris"'s door. She was very kind but the romance stuff ruined that. She didn't trust love either. We both got into pain games. My heart needs to heal of emotional pain. Theresa is looking for love. I must stop the lie. My wedding is over. Dot is over. I have Dan and Dave. I have the now of today. I am well. Why search the Philippines for love. Love is here in Sidney, Ohio. Theresa is being affectionate

9 Dec 05

Theresa is wonderful. We had a nice time last night. Called David and we are getting together for Christmas Lunch. This will be nice. I miss the boys…they are so fine. They are not little anymore. They are young men. Where has the time gone? My past is the past. I wish the divorce never happened but what can I do? I have the golf clubs and clothes and books that "Shelia" returned. This is the now. The wake of the boat cannot drive the boat forward. My pain is over. The past must stay past. Sad was the lunch with taxi cab driver and boys... so sad and lonely...but life moves on.

10 DEC 05

In my room I am safe...I miss my sons...life goes on...I continue to flirt on-line...the 946$ phone bill put an end to long distance...12 yrs married to Dorothy was a long time. My on-line flirt game won't fix that. I think I have family in Cebu City. Cold this winter's day. God is good. I am not manic...last year I was...thinking I was married to Audrey... how manic is that...2006 I will fly to Cebu and marry Belona. I am so lonely. My sons are in Beavercreek. There's nothing I can do about the divorce. Yvonne died and there's nothing I can do about that either. I'm safe in my room...no car... flirting on-line. Either I stay stateside with Theresa or go to Cebu city. $946 in phone calls is stupid. This will be a special Christmas. I must now mail my letters to the boys.

11 DEC 05

The internet is full of young girls wanting to marry rich American men. I try to stay real....Theresa is very sweet. Today our chat was very nice. Belona emailed stuff on marriage. Belona is very nice...but my sons are here. This is home. Cebu city Philippines is near China. What would my sons think of this. Dan and Dave are my flesh. They must come first.

12 DEC 05

Can't run off from the now. Must deal with divorce. Theresa is the now. My sons are here. I have old pictures of Dorothy and I. That is over. Must build on the now. Running off to the Philippines is not the right thing to do. The pain of the past is real. This will be a special

Christmas because of Theresa. We will build a fine day together. We spend hours talking together. We listen to music.

Why ruin that. Christmas will be just Theresa and I. I will call my son David. Oh well David isn't home.. I wonder if I will ever heal of my divorce. Yvonne wasn't given a fair chance because I wasn't over the divorce. The poor girl just wanted to be loved. We had a nice vacation together but drinking was a problem. The hotel was first class but Yvonne was drinking too much. We saw shows and ate dinner together. Why couldn't we enjoy each other. She had money. All Yvonne wanted was love. The vacation was nice. We were at Myrtle Beach. The shows were fun. I left Yvonne. I took the 1994 Honda Prelude. Now I'm sorry. Divorce hurts. Now I'm sorry I left Yvonne. I didn't give her a chance. How I wish I could do it over. I would love my wife. I must stop this running away. All my life I run away. I left home young. I hated my father…He didn't treat me right. Now I write him loving letters. "Sean" and I were 19 yrs old when we left home. Not a good thing.

This running away must stop. We took a bus to Illinois. It was stupid. After we got to Peoria he took all my money. Not a good thing.

Rent was due and I had no money. Leaving home was not a good thing. Mother sent $50 for Christmas. The card was sweet. I must treat Theresa better than Yvonne. I must grow up. Time now for Dollar General

16 DEC 05

I have shut down for a few days. It's Christmas Season and

Theresa is sad. I haven't heard from the boys. I will call them now. I hope to see them. Well the boys are not answering. I miss my sons. Many years ago when I went to see them I was depressed. I was sad. They had a big house and new cars and a new Dad. I ran away. I ran to Texas. I was very lonely. There I found myself on a VA Psych Ward. Well I'm done running away. Texas only made things worse. The car was taken back because payments were due. I found myself in a one-room apartment overlooking a golf course. I was sad. I was alone. I did stupid things to get attention. I stopped taking my meds. Somehow after that I was locked out and broke a window. I also walked the streets at night. These things were foolish. Today it would be foolish to leave Sidney, Ohio for the Philippines. Theresa is just down the hall and looks after me. I still am doing foolish things like giving out my address on the internet. This has got to stop as well as sending money out. Why am I not sending money to my sons? My doctors are here.

Why run away? When I was little I made cardboard wings and tried to fly away. Well it didn't work. Theresa will get up soon in her room and we can have coffee. This is real. This is my reality. These cardboard wings fly.

17 DEC 05

David called. Daniel and David and I are going out to lunch. I am so happy. It is good to talk to my son. Sometimes I wonder about my lost daughter…I mean my family is broken…today I will pay for lunch for the boys…it's the smallest thing. My sons are good to me.

Why do I give away money?? :Last night I vowed away more money. Just why am I doing this? Shouldn't I be helping my sons? Why am I doing this? My sons come first don't they?

Why do I vow away money. I fall for any hard luck story. Dan and Dave should be here soon.

20 DEC 05

The lunch with Dan and Dave was delightful…I now have Dave's email at school…I'm still a fool on the internet…but I'm getting more careful. I need to get right with God. On Christmas I will go to Holy Angels. I will be a better father to my sons. I will offer spending money to my sons because they are my sons.

31 DEC 05

Christmas was so special. Theresa put together a dinner. She got a black gold cross and pink flowers and cash. I sent cash to Ghana Africa and felt good about it. I love the spirit of giving. August 15, 2006 I'm marrying Belona in Cebu City Philippines. The boys called Christmas Day and they are getting flowers. This is a good year. 2006 will be even better.

1 JAN 06

Today is the first day of the rest of my life. Today I will take good care of myself. Today I will save my money. Today I will find God

5 JAN 06

I blew my check again and lied about it. I'm sick of this. I disconnected the DSL line. I sent Belona $450 and Ghana Africa $250.

Where is the savings? There is none. This must stop. I have nothing in the bank yet wrote a $300 check. This is stupid and must stop.

Let's change 2006. Let's save money. I want to fly to Cebu City and start over. I must save money and stop the stupid stuff

7 JAN 06

I must stop flying away. Theresa is wonderful. I build a life with Theresa. She is real. She puts up with everything. I start a new day today not in Cebu City. Divorce messed me up. I must stop flying away. Theresa is so kind and loving. Theresa is here. This is where I start. This is where I get better. I turned over the ATM card and credit card to Theresa. This summer I will play golf and bike. I will take my insulin shots. I will do something about my diet. Theresa is wonderful. Why am I giving her a hard time? My broken heart doesn't believe in real love. My broken heart wants to play hide and seek.. This is 2006. This year I heal my brokenness. Theresa is at Dollar General food shopping. I wish to show her the Journal. I wish to stop being stupid and start healing. The constant lying must stop. I must allow myself to be found. If I allow her she will ensure I save money. What is wrong with that? Why not trust Theresa who has proven trustworthy?

9 JAN 06

Theresa and I talked about the fact I screwed up my money again this month. I don't feel I deserve money. I feel unworthy. I give it away to others because I don't deserve it. This has gone on for years. Why not build my world on Theresa? Why not try to like me? I can stop being stupid. I can heal. I can ride my bike and play golf. What is wrong with me? I'm ok. I can heal. I know that I can live on a budget but this month I really messed it up. No more money sent to Belona. Theresa is here. This is reality. This is where I heal. David emailed me. He told me how Cebu City was a bad idea. He was right. I don't know Belona. The family would be disappointed.

It's dysfunctional. The event would be another fantasy into dysfunction. Flying away from reality. My son David is right. This is where I heal. This is where I get well.

12 JAN 06

David is dead set against Cebu City. I long for family. My mother and father are on their way out. My sons are grown. My room is small.

28 JAN 06

I want a wife. Theresa is willful. Belona is Asian submissive. Belona longs for a father to her children. This could be my Asian family.

Somehow my marriage to Dot must come to an end. Somehow I must move on. The concept of Asian escape appeals to me… a start over.

I want a new life. I want a better life. Maybe David will understand. My life is empty. I have no dream. Cebu City is my dream. This dream appeals to me. Cebu City attracts me to something more. I love Theresa . My interview with Manpower services was painful. I was a fool. I walked into a landmine. Well that's the story of my life. Cebu City could be a new start. I'm tired of being broken. I'm looking for wellness now. Something must mark an end to the divorce that haunts me. What is home? When do I find my way back home.??

I will go to confession today. I will confess sin against self. How worthless I feel.

30 JAN 06

Delightful necklaces arrived from   the Philippines.   This

summer I desire to marry Belona. I desire family. I desire Cebu City and a new way of life. This summer comes with it a tropical dream escape. A better way of life. I must do something to alter my wandering and aimless spirit. I desire my Cebu City family. I must admit I am charmed with Belona's Asian submissiveness. I am charmed with Cebu City. Wednesday I get paid. Feb 06 I must save my money. Bi-Polar is now controlled. I look to a new way of life. I am open to Cebu City. I must check it out and give it a try. I must see it on my terms. It must fit my needs and conditions.. I remember nothing of Dan and Dave. At 55 I desire the young body of Belona. This aimless spirit must find family. Must find direction and purpose. Isn't it every man's dream to find tropical escape in a new land. Belona's young body and pretty face and cute kids are attractive to me. Yes, this is radical. This is new. This is bold adventure. Leaving Dan and Dave will be hard. I desire to marry. The dream must go on. I guess I desire to be loved. I desire family and friends. Summer will come. I will marry. The adventure goes on.

20 Feb 06

David Emailed me, and my sons wanted to go to a driving range for golf. I was delighted to hear from my sons. Belona talks about her mother cooking for us and the !00$ apartment. It all sounds like a dream. Cebu City calls out to me. Doug talks about my life on the road. My life has been spent on the road. I know this may sound selfish but I must heal. I must save money. This month I did save money. Never have I done that before. Theresa has been a doll but I must look out for me first. I know how that must sound. The fact is simple. I am a failure as a husband and father. I understand this. Somehow this must be corrected. My faith has been shaken. My confession last month was delightful. Father was kind. He told me I was a man of faith.. Sex is a question. There must be no sex before marriage. Sex is sacred. As a Catholic this must be affirmed. I suppose in the end we must all love self. Why do I struggle with this issue of love of self? As a child I felt odd and lonely. This fact has haunted me all my life. In the end we return to our faith.   I mean what is this thing of a faith that has no forgiveness. . It sure does feel good to have money in the bank. Had a dream about David last night. I am without Dorothy because I hurt Dorothy. To hurt Theresa is not my aim.   To marry Belona is to marry her family. The cute 100$ apartment sounds like it would be delightful. Her Mother is so nice. I finished food shopping .

21 FEB 06

Talked with Belona.   I love her laugh.   She is so happy.. Theresa is so sad. Talked to the oldest child. She is a very cute girl. The two bedroom apartment is done Belona is sending pictures next week. 15 July 06 is still the target date to fly Cebu City.   Found out "Shelia" has tried to take other people's checks like mine. Why is it that I seem to find such people. A fool I must be to let other people take my money. I am warming up to the idea of marriage in Cebu City. I want to give it a shot. 937$ left in bank .This is a first for sure. 1 week to go and payday. I'm playing around with golf. The clubs are nice. The bank statement recorded western union. I blew a lot of money there for sure. Belona was so happy to hear my voice. Her sweetness is very nice. I love the idea of her mom cooking for us.

22 FEB 06

Talked with Belona. She is so playful. She needs money. Next month I will send some. I still have much left over. 200$ wont hurt.   Today is Theresa's birthday.   We are going to China Garden. I am not happy here. In Cebu I have an apartment. I have a family. Here I have very little. I see my boys once in awhile. I want to meet Belona.

25 Feb 06

David says he wants me to be there for him. Why am I supporting Belona and not David? I need to be there for David.

27 Feb 06

David never asks for money. He really loves me. He treats me well. He is a good son. We are going to try to meet this weekend

3 March 06

Doug called. My father is in the hospital for colon cancer. They found an ulcer. The doctor is not too worried. Ellen answered the phone. She is in charge. Tests coming in later this morning .I was worried. My father is central to my life. I'm glad we have patched things up.

I paid off phone today.   I've got $1000 in savings. I've got to level with my father. I must be a loving son. I went to the alcove when I got the news. I had steak and eggs as I do all the time. My father stirs me up. He is a part of me. A part of me misses him. Yet he provokes fights. He stirs up trouble. I've left messages for David. He says Sunday looks good for a visit. I will pay for the lunch and give out money for their gas and other expenses. My sons come first. My children must know they come first   Talking to Ellen was nice. I love my sister. I will call David again tomorrow. I am hoping Sunday works out. I will enjoy seeing them.

4 March 06

It does seem only right that my kids come first. Sunday I may see them. I will be generous. After paying phone bill I'm down to 1000$. I am waiting to see the pictures of the Cebu city apartment I just called Belona but no one is answering the phone. It's 6:24am. I must find a new way of life. I spend the day lying on Theresa's bed. This doesn't do. I must have a life. I wish to play golf. This could be a goal. I like golf. Who cares that I'm no good at it? I could get good if I put in the time. As a Catholic what do I have if not my faith. My faith has followed me all my life. It will guide me. My faith is showing me something about the good thing that saving money can bring. I saved 200$ on the phone bill by paying it off. This lesson is a first. The bank computer says 2000$. It's a new day. I'm learning. I'm paying off bills. Something must be done about the fact that there is always another girl. My father told me that. It's very true. There is always a girl. When there was no one I created Audrey. I was so lost that I even thought I was married to her. When you really get down to it who really cares about you? Mom cares about you. Dad cares about Dad. Mom has always been there for me. I still can't get thru to Belona. It's 7:41am. Belona is not home. David called. He got a job at a golf course. We are getting together today. I am delighted. David sounded happy. We can plan golf trips at Beavercreek. I haven't shot golf in a while. I'll have to start working on the short clubs first. If I take my time and work within my game it will be fun. Lunch with Dan and Dave was grand. We told tales of Mexico. I have forgotten many things. Maybe I wasn't so bad a father. I never was there and that I heard. Dave isn't listening to Cebu City stuff. He wants me here.

21 MARCH 06

Talked with Belona. She is quite cute. I will send her 400$ a month soon. Her TV is broke. She is bored. If she asks for 200$ she needs twice that number. I am staying away from Ken. He is going to get into trouble. I am not going to get into trouble. I took Ken and Tally and Leroy out to the China Garden. I loaned Ken $40. I'm going wild with the

ATM Card. The dinner was $45 Ken got $40. I will talk with Dad. I am going to take care of my ATM. I've got $75 left to payday. It's rubber check time again. When will I ever learn.

22 MARCH 06

Took $60 out of ATM. Found visa credit but it won't process. Going to bank today. Went to Rainbow last night. I thought it was sad watching all those people just drinking beer. There is $347 in visa. I could use $200 till payday. I processed Visa for $200. I'm all set now.

07 APR 06

Belona and I chatted and I find her quite cute and loving. Went to have dinner and listen to jazz. Things are looking up. Bills are being paid.

08 MAY 06

Have 300$ in savings…200$ checking…and still have 200$ in New York bank….things are picking up now…talked to Belona…she's such a doll so cute and loving….everything begins with cash in the bank….nothing happens without it… Mass this weekend was delightful…I realize how much I miss it…so much has changed since Holy Family School…I really should be doing confession every week…played the piano and loved it…the sound is very impressive…and reading poets and writers…I think of myself as a writer…

10 MAY 06

17 August 06 and I leave New York and I touch down at Cebu City at 11:30am…on the 19th of August. Just 2 more months and I'm finally there.

29 MAY 06

Get paid on the 1 June 06….book flight to Cebu in August…..
can't wait to finally get there and get married…..I totally blew
the checking account again…overdrawn by $350….when is
this going to end???

18ᵀᴴ JUNE 06

Father's Day with no word from my sons…they must be mad
at me….got upset and left two emotionally abusive calls on
Dave's cell phone. Not a good idea. I learned this emotional
abuse from Dad…who learned this emotional abuse from his
Dad.

Dearest Son David

I am so sorry that I yelled in the record of your cell phone
because Dan never calls or writes…I sent very nice and
expensive flowers on Easter and never got a reply and that
hurt me deeply . Telling you Dan is toast was not a very good
idea. Oh well such is the breaks of life. I now go to the
Catholic mass at "Holy Angels" and the Christian rock service
at 1ˢᵗ Methodist Church at Sidney. The 2 punch effect of this
spiritual event is profound. The Catholic Church has the
liturgy and the Eucharist…and Sidney Methodist First has the
worship and fellowship.

20ᵀᴴ JUNE 06

Dearest Son Dan and David

It was a hard snow day back in the early 60's…I was attending
Holy Family School in Hicksville New York…my father had
just told us not to talk to strangers…I was walking right in
front of my house…and a car pulled up…a man opened the
window and asked me if I wanted to earn five bucks to shovel

snow from his driveway…"Sure". I said.   We drove and drove all over Long Island…finally we were a very long way from home. He pulls up to his "house". There is a for sale sign on his lawn. There is a baseball bat in the back seat. He unzipped his pants and asks me if I want 5 bucks to touch his penis.   I scream and dive out of the car into the snow. He backs up to hit me and I dive into a snow bank on the sidewalk off the road. He takes off. I cry down the block. A very nice old lady invites me in for cookies and milk. She calls the cops. The cops come and drive me to station. In the station the cops talk to me… finally one cop has to go to the bathroom…I follow. When he unzipped his pants I freak. The detectives then talk to me. All I know is that their weapon is a Smith and Wesson .38.. I am driven home then and my father and mother talk with the cops. Nothing is done. I receive no therapy for this very traumatic event in my young life.

Years latter when I saw the weapons of the cops in the Air Force I knew I just had to have those weapons. Once getting them I was a crack shot. No one was going to screw with me again and get away with it. My nickname was Sgt Killer. I was deadly. I loved every minute

After the divorce that was final in 1988…I was totally broken…I seized the engine on the Toyota that mom had given me. I was a mess driving all over town not knowing where to go. I hooked with "Cris" who only added to my blood and pain axe murdered heart. I never asked sex yet paid all her bills. In 1992 when you moved to Beavercreek Ohio…I found your Abbey gate…brick two-story $500K house. I had $90 bucks to my name and no car. Your new step-father had my sons, my ex-wife, and 3 new cars parked in front of his house…couldn't take it…. So in 1994, I took the new Honda Prelude from my wife Yvonne and later on went to Laredo Texas to cross the border and find love.   Drove 3 days non-stop. When I got to Laredo I realized that I was manic again. Parked red Honda 1994 Prelude that my wife Yvonne paid for…in front of local hospital. Once there had the doctors see my Air Force ID. I was transferred to La Rosa. This private psych hospital was manna from heaven. No VA Psych ward this one. I was in awe of the Plexiglass intense psych ward…no steel. The nurse wore cute uniforms relaxed and the Zen fishpond in back of hospital awesome. Never, never, never, did I want this heaven to end. Infuriatingly when my insurance would no longer pay I was back in the San Antonio VA Medical Center.

Oh shit. Shit Happens.

June 06

Dearest Dan and Dave

I have always been a freak for fire. My best buddy… "Sean" and I went to ice pond to fish. We were under the bridge. I fell into the frozen ice water…"Sean" built a fire and I stripped to underwear. The fire warmed my soul in the cold, cold air. God, I love fire. Years later in the early 1990's I had a duplex in Portsmouth Virginia. The back yard was a mess. I raked all the leaves and stuff. Started a huge fire that I danced all around until the firemen came to see what the hell I was doing. I had a blast dancing around my huge fire.

23ʳᵈ June 06

Dearest Dan and Dave

"the thorazine kid"

I was so loaded on thorazine that I had the thorazine shuffle. This anti-psychotic was so potent that it was very low maintenance…

There was no way now that I was going to be a problem to

anyone…I was a walking vegetable. I then took over the ping pong table with a yellow ping pong ball as the "thorazine kid". I was so lost in my own world I just couldn't be beaten on that table with my yellow ball..

When I got a level four…I took over the pool table in the basement. I still love pool but never bet money on it. I may sometimes play for a "bud" Never , never, never whiskey. I really shouldn't be drinking "bud" but 2 is my limit. A man must know his limits. I didn't labor day 1980 and that's what started this manic mess stuff. I totally burnt off…because I didn't respect myself enough to know my limits

24TH JUNE 06

Dearest Dan and Dave

The daffy duck derby was fabulous…Hits 105.5 was there. It was a blast with free food. A huge crane lifted a wooden cage with a trap door 100 feet in the air. At the apex of the lift the trap door flew open and hundreds of rubber ducks hit the Miami River . My rubber duck did not win. I had a blast. The Mexican food at the battle of the bands was delightful… Theresa and I are going to go and have another taste. In the late 1960's I was in a band called "These". Don and Johnny and I had a lot of fun. I played an accordion that was electric. I was always forgetting the chords. Don played guitar…and Johnny played drums. We had a lot of fun but I think I drove them nutz.

26TH JUNE 06

Dearest Dan and Dave

In the early 1960's my father took the family water-skiing on Long Island Sound. The prop sheared and I fell in a school of jellyfish. It was delightful. They were in my face and hair and all over my back. In the late 1960's your mother and I would go to Bayard's Arboretum on Long Island. The geese filled the front lawn. Indian artifacts were on display. The flowers and trees were awesome. Ask Mom about it. Later in the 1970's your mom and I went to what was then Salisbury Park   to an anti-war candle light service. No one then that I knew wanted Vietnam.   My hero was John Lennon. I worshiped the Beatles.

It was 1987, when I crossed the border to Mexico with a Spanish-American dictionary to order food and learn the language, that I discovered Mexico. This was during my separation from your mother. The divorce was finalized in 1988. I loved Mexico.

7 JULY 06

Dearest Dan and Dave

Grandma's ducks at Baldwin, New York were cool. She had a pond in her back yard. She fed them and the bluejays stale bread everyday.

She fed me lean red roast beef sandwiches on fresh German bread.   The blueberry pie was awesome with white sugar dusted on top.

I hope you hear your Father's voice in the fish swimming in the stream, and listen to His sound on the waves, in the ocean. I hope you visit Mother Earth today in her living bio-mass, as you watch all her creation. Soon I shall be leaving to Philippines, to go on with the next phase of my life. My wife to be, Belona , needs me to help her with the kids. I get a second chance to get fatherhood right this time. I do not hear from you, and that is very sad. I did get an email on father's day. That was awesome. I will be coming back to visit America once a year after the 10th of August 06.

13 JULY 06

Dear Dan and Dave

I have handed over to Theresa my passport and tickets to the Philippines. This delusion must stop. I am going nowhere. I am going to learn to be a good father to my sons. I left home at 17 and I have not stopped running away. I plan on setting up an apartment that I can call home. We will stir-fry with my wok and your mother's spice rack. This wok and spice rack will be home. Right now, I am in a room. Soon I will advance my quest for a better life. It starts here in Sidney, where I came to reside 8 yrs ago. It will end in Sidney. I bury myself at the VA in Dayton. I have insight now what a father does. He stands firm for his sons. That is what I am going to do. My sons come first

28 JULY 06

Dear Dan and Dave.

Well, I haven't heard from you guys in a month, but I know you're busy. I plan on being right here for you. I know we will see each other soon. I can still try to be a better father. It's not over yet. I can always learn.

1 AUGUST 06

Dear Dan and Dave,

Today I called you but hung up after 3 rings knowing the trouble it would cause calling your Mother's house after the events of last year. Oh well, must just hang tough, and wait till you contact me…calling your house is a very bad idea and I know it….I must leave your mother alone…I've caused enough trouble…last year…when I went psychotic and caused a scene.

19 AUGUST 06

Theresa and I signed a lease on a new 2 Bedroom Apt. It's just delightful. Theresa will have a huge new kitchen to cook from. It's got central air and a wonderful patio. It's on the 3rd Floor. A home at last. This is good. On Christmas this year we can have a tree. Things are looking up. Theresa and I are getting along fine as long as I respect her boundaries. God is good. My broken heart is healing. I know that my sons love me, and they are busy.

25 AUGUST 06

I must stop running away. I'm listening to the CD that Dad gave me when I went to my last psych ward. Sidney is my home. The new apartment is home. I must stop running away. This Christmas, I will be in the new apartment, and healing my broken heart. I remember the falling rain, and no place to go. Homeless and alone, is no more. I am getting well. Soon, I will see my sons. We will dine at Lee's Chinese, and play golf. God is Good.

LABOR DAY 2006

I saw Fr Jerry for confession on Sat and went to Mass on Sunday. 26 yrs ago this adventure into manic psychosis started. I never asked for the trip. This Oct I will see Mom and Dad. I don't know how long I will have them.

15 SEPTEMBER 2006

The move has gone well. The apt is now furnished with old stuff and a delightful couch. I finally have a home. I have stopped being a big flirt. Theresa and I enjoy a romantic event every night but sex is not in our game plan. Last night I was up at 2am. I just couldn't sleep without my anti-psychotic that I ran out of. I slept in Theresa's arms. I have cut off all the delusion's of the Philippine's. I am letting my sons come back to me, when they are ready.

MILITARY HAZING

My hazing started the first day I reported to my post at the Military Airlift Command. I was an Elite Guard Troop of the 375th Security Police Squadron. Sgt Hall radioed me to respond to the 3rd Floor of the command. The joke of this event was to get me totally lost in the command.

Of course I did . The hazing continued because my wife was an officer and I was living in officer housing. The next event was the day I was at my post and got a call from base relocation, that orders had been cut for my remote assignment to the Aleutian Islands. I freaked out. It's a horrid place 60 below zero without family. The flight had a big joke of this. The next event was to try to get me written up. I was indoctrinated never to unsnap my weapon unless it was to be used in deadly force. Sgt Slack pulled an exercise. The command post was penetrated and we were to respond to neutralize this security breach. Sgt Slack showed up at my post with his weapon drawn. He was testing me to see if I would draw my weapon, so he could write me up. By far the worst event was the day the flight transferred the radio network to me as the alternate radio network. This was done at midnight and I was not trained, I was a green troop, and the joke was to pull a "looking glass" exercise that there was no way I could handle. I freaked out at the command post much to the delight of the flight. The joke wasn't so funny when 2 troops took their live from the stress of the flight. One troop toke the police shotgun from his police car, put it to his chest, and pulled the trigger. When I broke into "borderline psychosis" everyone covered their ass. Suddenly my cross training paperwork when through and I reported to the Military Airlift Command Management Engineering Team. When I got there the games stopped and I was treated as a professional, since my degree was in Industrial Technology. However, my mind never healed from borderline psychosis and when I broke a second time at the National Prayer Breakfast, that was the end of my Military Career.

17 SEPTEMBER 2006

Psychotherapy, at Aspen Wellness Center, is going very well. I shower every day, brush my teeth 3 times a day, wear clean clothes and do my Zen Relaxation and Zen Meditation everyday. I have increased my medication to help me sleep. The last few nights I have not slept. I enjoyed a good bike ride on my Mongoose. Zen is helping me but Zen is something that I found many years ago and have returned to. My therapist suggested 8 minute meditation which is very good. I am now meditating 1 hour a day. Today is Sunday and I will attend Holy Angels Mass at 10:30am. The Pope gave at great speech which has caused a great outcry from Islam where many took the speech out of context.

19 SEPTEMBER 2006

I called the University of Dayton about a Master's of Computer Science. I really would like to do this. The apt is doing well. Art hung on walls. Theresa and I getting along very well. Psychotherapy going well.

06 OCT 06

Psychotherapy going very well at Aspen Wellness Center. I now realize the emotional pain my father has put me through. I just wrote my sister a letter basically saying I wasn't going to take anymore shit from my father. The yelling and screaming and provoking fights is crap.

At 56 yrs I don't have to put up with that anymore. Still have not heard a word from the boys since father's day. Theresa and

I are planning a delightful Christmas together at the house. I am staying clear of pain. I don't deserve or need pain. I've stopped email to

Belona, because I am not going there to marry her or adopt her kids or anything else. I am staying here and continuing to get well.

It will take a long time to correct my credit history, which reflects my manic spending. My birthday is Oct 11 and still no cards in the mail. Theresa is out walking to Krogers for food shopping and I am going to settle into a good Tom Clancy book.

14 Oct 06

I am trying to get the medical reports from the Dayton VA Medical Center for my work. Theresa and I had a delightful birthday dinner of steak and Chinese salad. I ordered more Tom Clancy books today. The birthday party is planned for Sunday at 2:00 pm.

Today ate at the "Bistro" and Jennifer served me a delightful strip steak dinner. Absolutely wonderful.

15 Oct 06

The birthday party was a huge success. We all had a wonderful time. Theresa made a strawberry cake. I hope the pictures come out well so that I can send some to Douglas. Well, back to dinner and salad. God Bless All those like me who find the Mass a thing of art.

16 October 2006

Somehow when you are divorced and dumped you feel marked as damaged goods. This feeling of rejection at the hands of your wife is very painful and takes years to recover from. I now accept the divorce and realize that Theresa is best friend, and our friendship can overcome my painful divorce. The one thing I am sure of is that psychotherapy and confession and Mass on Sunday as well as following doctor's orders is keeping me from manic episodes. The neatness and modern apartment is also a factor in my favor. My life is taking shape and order. This is good. My Zen Catholic faith is good. I love now a healthy routine. I have not returned to the chaos of manic psychosis and the hell it brought into my life. One thing that I must work on now is living on a budget. When I go over budget this hurts me fiscally. This is an old habit hard to outlive.

17 OCTOBER 2006

This eating out habit of mine has got to stop. I blow the budget all the time doing this stuff. I can go to Food Town and eat well at home.

18 OCTOBER 2006

I was depressed today over the fact that I have not heard from my sons since father's day. This is something that I cannot do anything about.

I pay off Visa 1 Nov 06 and it is going to stay paid off. I must reframe from always going into debt. This old habit is hard to kill off.

My therapist at "Aspen Wellness Center" gave me a birthday card which I thought was very nice.

19 OCTOBER 2006

Theresa came back from food shopping last night and we ate

spaghetti. How nice it is to be stable. This is not a delusion of the Philippines.

This is real. Today I will be studying for the written exam of my Ohio license. Getting an Ohio license and car will go a long way towards my independent living. I am now wasting money on little things. 1 November I pay off Visa and give the card to Theresa so that it stays paid off.

20 OCTOBER 2006

When will I finally get it? I mean spending only what I have? The extra $400 to the DMV in Virginia really hit me hard. Oh well I must look carefully about spending money till I get paid. This shouldn't be too hard. The quality of my friendship with Theresa is delightful. We are getting along just fine. My life is boring but stable, so I guess you can't ask for everything, at least not at once anyhow. My credit history is very poor, according to Equifax anyhow. Well, when you're manic, you're manic. But I guess that doesn't count with those people anyhow. My home has become my "safe haven". I look forward to fixing it up with kitchen and other stuff. The apartment complex is shaping up quite well now. Well, I kind of over ate today. Guess you pay the price for that sort of thing. You just can't rush a journal like this. I find many things to revise. The thing to do is buy a used car first, and then a new computer, and then finally send this journal off to the editor.

22 OCTOBER 2006

I spent $200 on eating out this month, and $400 to the DMV of Virginia for fines. I now have $40 in the checking account and I've got 10 days till payday. Some things just don't change. I'm taking the driver's exam on Thursday. Early in November I will take the road test. I am looking forward to an Ohio

Driver's License. Maybe next month I will finally not blow my check. That would be nice, for a change.

23 OCTOBER 2006

I haven't heard from the boys since father's day. This makes me sad, but there is little I can do about it. Oh well, if they don't want to talk to me there is little I can do about it. Maybe they will change their minds. Meanwhile I am taking my meds and staying out of trouble. I am depressed about the boys, but I must go on with my life.

26 OCTOBER 2006

The credit reporting agencies are giving me a hard time over correcting my ruined credit. They are not fair and could not care less that when I was manic, I was manic and ruined my credit. Basically it's an uphill fight. I have stopped abusing my Visa credit card. Finally and very slowly I am taking charge of my ruined credit. In November I am set on finally taking charge of my constant overspending. Every month it's the same thing. I am broke at the end of the month. Well, at least I have stopped giving money away. This is good. I guess bad habits are hard to break. I dump on myself. How stupid. We all have problems to overcome. I admire the fact that Theresa always saves her money. I wish I could be more like this. I have settled upon the fact that Lexington Law Firm will dispute my ruined credit, and this process is not a quick fix. I have also settled upon the fact that my sons are young men with there own lives to live. If they do get in touch that would be delightful, but if they don't, they don't, and that's life. Today I will continue the dispute process with letters, and study for the written drivers exam. I am going to stop dumping upon me. I've been manic many years, and that's life. You play the cards that you are dealt. When I get paid on the 1ˢᵗ I can stop my manic spending and live a more stable life with my money. I can learn to save like Theresa saves.

Tonight is spaghetti dinner night. I walked in the rain and mailed off my letters of dispute to the credit reporting agencies. It's so nice to have a home. It's so nice to be well. Well, the big test is coming on the 1ˢᵗ, and we will see if I can save my check and not blow it like in October and September. I will study now for my driver's written exam.

29 OCTOBER 2006

Sometimes, I remember the old days of Dorothy. I wish she was still my friend. That is long past. Somehow I must get on with my life. Yet, the old days linger on my mind. Life is quiet and stable now after many years of manic stuff. I have trouble recalling all the manic stuff now. Yet, it happened and was very unstable. Theresa is very supportive. Last night I watched a Tai Chi DVD. The old actor of the classic TV series "Kung Fu" directed the DVD. I realized how old he was. This made me feel old. Well, I have aged. Life goes on. My life is better now. Someone has pulled the fire station box in the apartment complex. How stupid is this?

30 OCTOBER 2006

Theresa and I are getting along just fine. I have to adjust to the times. I'm 56 now. I am retired. My life is stable. My father's printer will work fine on my computer, Doug says. So that will be nice. The usual scams are filling my mailbox. I still have not heard from my sons. It will take months to rebuild my credit. Well, I will listen to Jazz now.

31 OCTOBER 2006

It seems like such a bad dream. Homeless, flying space available all around the Air Force bases. At Wright-Patterson

AFB I would sleep in the mens' room. In Dayton, I would give blood and then buy bread and bologna. At least now I finally have a home. Andrews AFB, was the worst. I of course had no car and walked everywhere. Christmas at Norfolk VA Navel Base, was very lonely. "Cris" just dropped me off at the base. I can think of nothing worse than being mentally ill and homeless. Divorce can be cruel. The holidays are horrid. At the San Antonio VA Medical Center, I bought a cup of coffee and wrote Christmas letters. This year Theresa and I are buying a Christmas Tree for the house. Homeless in Dayton, I would leave St Vincent's shelter early in the morning and hang out at the public library. Once I slept on a heating grate at the Hertz car rental building in Dayton and got robbed of my cash, but I hid my stash of cash in my shoe. It is so nice now to have Theresa. She makes the apartment a real home. When I get my license, I will not drive outside of Sidney. Not without Theresa. Once, I remember Danville, VA. I was searching for my late wife Yvonne. I walked all over town. My head was sun burnt and I sat in a gas station pouring cold water on my head. At nightfall I had to leave. Two kids in the night came upon my back , and tried to push me off a bridge. Thank God, I hit the guard rail. Later I was picked up by the police, on a stupid bullshit warrant that "Susan" took out on me, just to be mean for leaving her. My back hurt lying in a concrete jail floor. Thank God no one ever really hurt me. Now I just want to stay out of trouble and stay home.

BOOK TWO

——————— Chapter One ———————

Dayton VA Medical Center

---

1 November 2006

Went to Aspen Wellness Center and saw my therapist. It was a good session. Well, this is a new month, and I'm not going to mess up my account. I feel my progress of stability is a step by step process. Little steps lead to bigger steps. I called Ellen twice yesterday but in vain, for she was not home. The fridge is full of food.

2 November 2006

The following is discharge summary and progress note of the Dayton VA Medical Center

DISCHARGE SUMMARY page 3 admin date: Aug 31, 2004 discharge date Sept 10, 2004, attending Walters, Charles L

Chief Complaint: "I was in the elite corps from 1978 to 1981"

History of present illness: The patient is a 53- year old white male who was admitted to 7 south on August 31, 2004 for mania. He said that a Jewish doctor programmed him to kill his catholic wife. He denied having any suicidal and homicidal ideation. He denied using alcohol and drugs.

3 NOVEMBER 2006

DISCHARGE SUMMARY page 5 admin date Sept 14, 2000 discharge date Sept 27 2000, attending Harrison, Judith A

Reason for admission: The patient admitted to Dayton VAMC Nursing home Care Unit on 9/14/00 for respite care. He resides in a group residential home. He will be discharged home on 9/27/00. He denies any complaints. He denies hallucinations or suicide ideation

DISCHARGE SUMMARY page 7 admin date June 07, 1998 discharge date July 1, 1998 attending Adityanjee

AXIS 1 Bi-Polar disorder, manic, with mood congruent psychotic features. Treatment non-compliance.

AXIS 2 Narcissistic, dependent and passive aggressive personality traits

Temporary homelessness

Presenting complaints: "The patient presented to Fairborn police, with complaints of being depressed and suicidal, who brought him to the emergency room."

This 47 – year – old white male was last hospitalized at Dayton VA Medical from 05/07/98 to 5/26/98. The patient was transferred to domiciliary on same day, where he left without permission and was given an irregular discharge on 06/01/98. The patient appears to have been noncompliant with medication leading to relapse of his symptoms. The patient states that he has not been taking his medications regularly and has spend more than $2,000 in the past one week on food, entertainment, including women. The patient reports feeling high, increasing energy decreased sleep, racing thoughts, and talking too much. The patient claims to have been hearing voices of God. He states that on the day prior to admission he felt suicidal and therefore, went to the police at Fairborn Police Station who brought him to the VA hospital.

The patient was admitted to 7- south ward under the care of Dr. Adityanjee and was put on level one, suicidal precautions. He was reviewed by the treatment team on 06/08/98.

On mental state examination, he was found to be a white male with clean shaven head, wearing dark glasses and hospital pajamas. He had increased psychomotor activity. He maintained good eye contact. Speech was pressured. He had delusions about secret service and air force base. He denied any suicidal ideas but volunteered in a playful and jocular mood . Patient was alert, conscious and oriented. He lacked insight and judgment sense. In view of the lack of suicidal ideas, suicidal precaution was discontinued . The patient was started back on lithium, depakote and olanzapine. Over a period of time, the patient started to show improvement. The social worker, Mr. Hugger, got in touch with the patient's brother in New York City. The patient was cooperative with ward rules and regulations. He participated in the treatment plan and insisted that he wanted to be closer to his 2 sons rather than go back to New York. His family members, especially his mother and brother, also insisted that initially he has to be stable before they will try to help him in the New York area with his finances as well as with his home placement. Therefore, the plan to transfer him back to New York was shelved and it was decided to place the patient locally in some group home. The team also decided to contact his ex-wife to arrange a family meeting and Mr. Hugger, the social worker, sent a letter to this effect to his ex-wife.

The patient agreed to be discharged to a group home in Sidney, OH and was visited by some screens from their facility. In view of his poor medication compliance, it was decided to start the patient on injection Prolixin Decanoate. Meanwhile, the patient's family in New York decided to assume financial power of attorney responsibility and were willing to advance money for group home placement. The patient was accepted for Sidney RCH Veteran's Home, 414 South Main Ave, Sidney 45365. It was decided that the patient will close his bank account locally and that his benefit check will be returned back to his New York account, to his mother who will manage his money. The patient agreed for this arrangement. On the day of discharge, his former wife Mrs. Dorothy Clark, came for a meeting with the Treatment Team. The treatment team explained to her the patient's desire for close touch with his 2 sons. His former wife explained that unless he complies with his medication and does not display any inappropriate behavior his children would not be willing to meet with him.

DISCHARGE SUMMARY page 13 admin date May 07, 1998 discharge date May 26, 1998 attending Adityanjee

Chief Compliant : " I was staging a protest"

This 47 year old while male, married, but divorced, living by himself, was last hospitalized at Dayton VA Medical Center from 4/10/98 to 4/28/98/ Subsequently, the patient was transferred to the domiciliary. He had an irregular discharge from domiciliary within three days of transfer there and was living by himself and was reportedly noncompliant with medications.

The patient was brought to the VAMC ER on 5/07/98 by Fairborn Police for creating a public disturbance at Wright-Patterson AFB. The patient states that he has been barred from entering the base because "his wife is black". The patient was subsequently admitted to 7 south under the care of Dr. Adityanjee.

Worked in the USAF in 1978 and had an honorable discharge. He is 100% service connected.

He was a tall white male with a shaved head, dressed in hospital pajamas with increased psychomotor activity, pressured speech, irritability, and possible persecutory delusions towards the United States Government. The patient had some insight into his mental illness and regrets leaving the dom in an irregular manner. The patient was somber about the handling of his life over the last year. He did not have grandiose or persecutory delusions, therefore it was decided to go ahead with a PRP consult. The patient expressed the idea of going back to New York, as he felt ashamed having made a nuisance of himself to the Fairborn police, but when the implications of return to New York and the issue of his mother controlling his finances were discussed, he realized that it would be short-term solution for his overall psychiatric problems and the way he has handled them.

This 47 – year old white male was admitted to the domiciliary after hospitalization. While he was living out in the community, the vet became noncompliant with his medication and suicidal, therefore, was admitted to the Tower for stabilization. Upon stabilization, the vet was admitted to the dom to further stabilize him taking medications prior to his returning to residential care home in Fairborn, OH at the Hope House and does owe them some back monies and he will make arrangements for this payment. On the weekend of 5/01/98 to 5/04/98 it appears that the vet left the section and he failed to return, therefore making his own living arrangements in the community. This vet, per day treatment team, is given an irregular discharge effective 5/04/98.

DISCHARGE SUMMARY page 16 admin April 10, 1998 discharge date April 28, 1998 Attending Adityanjee

Chief Compliant: " I came for protection. I am priority A."

This 47 – year old white male, married but separated, living by himself up to 2 days ago, was admitted via ER. The patient has the diagnosis of bi-polar disorder and his last admission in the psychiatric unit was 3/02/98 to 3/13/98. The patient was unable to give a detailed history at the time of his admission and the MOD noted the conversation as follows, "are you aware of what treason means, I have only been tortured for 28 yrs. How much of my blood has been drawn and sold in the market? Do you know how word Washington is spelled? I am not talking. I observed on the television screen blood and destruction. It was very shocking. Let us get back to original transmission. Blood is sacred.

There is only one faith. That is America. The cow is sacred. It provides mother's milk. The soil is sacred. It provides food You cannot live without water. God is a toy and is not sacred but human life is. I studied religion. I am not a fool you think I am. Have you ever heard of Abraham Lincoln" The patient started to laugh. The patient shows distractibility, flight of ideas, pressure of speech, labile mood with incongruity with tendencies to interfere with staff. He is unable to hold a conversation on one theme.

The patient was diagnosed with bi-polar disorder in 1981. He has had multiple psychiatric admissions including recent one in Feb/Mar , 1998 in 7 south under the care of Dr. Adityanjee. He reports having made a suicide attempt in 1994. The patient has been noncompliant with his medication since the discharge from 7 south. He admits to drinking wine occasionally which might contribute to frequent noncompliance.

The patient was highly preoccupied with secrets of intelligence activities and talked about code name of President Bush. He continued to be delusional and expressed abusive thoughts toward his own physician's ethic origin.

DISCHARGE SUMMARY page admin 23 March 02, 1998 discharge 17, March 1998 Attending Adityanjee

Presenting Compliant: "Came to Wright Patterson AFB medical center for medication and stabilization because they are the best"

This patient is a 47 – year old white 100% serive-connected male vet with a history of established bi-polar disorder. The patient presented to the ER of the Wright Patterson AFB medical center on the day before admission with the complaints of "my medications needs stabilization, I know I am manic, I know I have to slow down, my engine is running at 550 RPM. If an engine races it boils over then it seizes". The patient stopped taking his medications apparently 5 days prior to admission. He was assessed in the Wright Patterson AFB medical center walk in clinic and found to be manic with religious, philosophical , and theological preoccupation. He was distractible and had flight of ideas, pressured speech and euphoric mood. The patient attempted suicide in 1994. He is separated from second wife who has paranoid schizophrenia. He reports some verbal abuse from his father during early childhood.

The patient was very cooperative as far as management of his hypo manic symptoms were concerned, however, he continued to be elated, euphoric , with increase psychomotor activity. He manifested numerous grandiose delusions and believed that he was doing some research work at Wright-Patterson AFB and claimed that it was secret. He showed jocular and playful behavior.

Gradually over a period of time, his elation and jocularity subsided. He no longer manifested grandiose delusions and developed adequate amount of insight into his symptoms. The vet did not want to go back to New York and his group home, therefore the social worker got in touch with his mother who also had the financial power of attorney as well as with his case manager, Mr Demato, from the New York Community

Mental Health Center. After discussing it with him, his mother, case manager, and the patient it was decided that vet can continue to stay in the Dayton area as he was reluctant to go back to New York. However, vet was persuaded to go to a group home. The patient was accepted for placement to Hope House and was discharged there on 3/17/98

DISCHARGE SUMMARY page 27 admin date 15 May 1997 discharge date 22 May 1997 Attending Adityanjee

Mr. Keller is a 46 – year old white male with a chief compliant of "I made an error in judgment when I chose not to continue Clonazepam"

He has history of bi-polar disorder which was diagnosed in 1981. He presented to the VAMC with the intention of hospitalization for management of bipolar disorder. He stated that he chose not to continue taking his Clonazepam but to continue taking lithium and depakote 2 weeks ago. He reported poor sleep consisting of 2 or 3 hours of sleep per night stating "this means that I'm one step away from hospitization", he reports good medical compliance for 2 yrs.

The patient is from out of state and has been followed at the Northport VA, New York. He has been in Dayton since early March visiting his children from his 1st marriage. Several days ago he attended a National Police convention at Wright-Patterson AFB and states that he "went off" during the exercise and states " the police descended on me". He reports being arrested, detained and released. He also stated that he was involved with security police in the AFB 3 times on the day of admission for "bizarre behavior". He was brought in the evening admission by the Air Force Base Squad members. The vet acknowledged the fact that he needs help. He has decreased sleep, increased energy, racing thoughts, irate behavior, feelings of entering depression, feelings of being "saturated" with certain topics, no change in libido, decreased appetite, feelings of hostility/ disliking of women, suicidal ideation without plan, no homicidal ideation

The vet was hospitalized at the VAMC in Dayton June 27, 1994 through July 8, 1994 with diagnosis of bipolar disorder, manic phase. His bipolar disorder was diagnosis in 1981. He has been seen by Dr. Tolatino at the Northport VA outpatient clinic. He has a history of suicide attempt by drug overdose in 1994.

He has been married twice. He has 2 children from the first marriage. The vet is separated from his 2nd wife who has paranoid schizophrenia. He was verbally abused as a child. He states " I was a misunderstood child"

He reported sleepiness, trouble remembering things and disruptive and erratic behavior at the Wright Patterson AFB the day prior. He did appear to be grandiose during the interview and told the treatment team that he was given experimental drugs while he was in the air force. He just related that he was administered LSD in 1981 while on active duty and his biggest mistake was not taking his medications. He was friendly and pleasant to his peers and very amenable to treatment.

On 5/18/97 the vet was happy and reported that he has now been able to sleep. He was very pleasant and did not have any complaints.

He has been spending a lot of money on a woman with a daughter with sickle cell disease that he had not previously known. He described concern about his wife who he describes as a paranoid schizophrenic, alcoholic and extremely suicidal. He is concerned because she has begun to drink again.

The vet met with the treatment team on 5/20/97 and reported continued improvement in sleep, decreased activity, decreased racing thoughts. The vet did state that he felt that he had enough money to pay for his apartment when discharged. The vet was very cooperative throughout his hospital stay with is treatment plan and taking his medications. He showed continued improvement on 5/21/97 and stated that he felt ready to be discharged. He plan was to stay with a friend in Fairborn, Ohio after discharge. His manic symptoms had resolved prior to discharge.

PROGESS NOTE page 35 Dayton VAMC entry date Sept 29, 2006 Author: Walters, Charles L

Subjective:
Patient continues to do well on meds. He is writing a book and thinking about getting his Master's Degree at UD.

PROGRESS NOTE page 45 Dayton VAMC entry date: Sept 09.2004 Author Harris , David A

The patient, Keller, Kevin J, is being discharged from acute psychiatry unit 7 south 9/10/04. The vet will follow up with Dr. Walters in the MHC for his mental health needs. Vet will be transported by VA transportation to his home at 121 Beech St. in Sidney, Ohio, 45365

Vet is sitting in the front T.V. lounge " I know they programmed me to kill my catholic wife. The words are spot, dot, red. President Bush came to Sidney to the Spot restaurant and the white house advance team activated my code words. Vet remains delusional and paranoid. Alteration in thought process r/t psychosis and delusions. Vet rambled on about his belief that the Government has programmed him to kill his wife and the three code words that signify this plan. Patient stated that this occurred in 1980. Vet describes himself as a type of operative. Vet states he was banned from WPAFB due to chasing a guard around the area whom he thought was part of the plan due to a red hat she had on. Vet remains hypomanic, loud and sudden vocalizations, Continue Level one. Monitor.

Continues to be manic, hyper verbal with loose associations as he states, " I am here for deprogramming. I am not effective."

Pt ambulating unit singing, had to be asked to lower his voice, pt complied. Pt continues to refer to "code words". Talked with Chaplain for extended period this shift. Participated in social activity, was appropriate. Currently in dayroom watching TV

Pt low-key this shift. Has been in room or in dayroom watching tv. Minimal interaction with staff/peers. Pt came to nurses' station this afternoon "Strategic plans are executed with code words. Thank you ma'am.

Vet's mood is hypo manic and grandiose with some rambling speech. He has been dropping off bizarre notes at the nurses' station that make no sense.

Audrey Willis is the person who is renting a room to Mr. Kevin J. Keller. She came to visit pt yesterday evening and wanted to leave her phone number and address in case somebody here wants to get in touch with her.

PROGRESS NOTE page 55 Dayton VAMC entry date Sept 01, 2004 Author Altman , Susan

Vet has been up and about the unit. Continues to be manic/euphoric. Vet states that he has been programmed to kill his Catholic wife.

Vet called and left a message with the Patient Advocate stating that he had been programmed to kill my wife" patient states he wants the advocate to represent him...the message was forwarded to police...police states while patient is inpt...

this comment falls under the Tarriff act and the wife must be notified…police will notify the wife of the possible threat on her life.

The vet was brought to this VA on a 72 hr hold by Sidney police because he had HI toward his ex-wife. The pink slip by Dr. Tenneyck indicated that he went to the police station with a note that said he was programmed to kill his wife. At the time he was "hyper manic" with tangential thoughts about being programmed and activated today"

Vet told treatment team that General Huyser sent him to an Indian Dr. and the Dr. programmed him to kill his wife, and he wants to sue for 2 zillion dollars. He said he has an access code to the white house and talked about the "advance team". He said, " I don't want to hurt my ex-wife, I want to kiss her."

PROGRESS NOTE page 61 Dayton VAMC entry date Aug 31, 2004 Author: Martin, Christine

53 year old, white, male, service connected 100% c/o psychotic for past 18 yrs. Pt states the police were involved to put him in "protective custody" so he wouldn't hurt self or others. Pt vehemently denies SI, HI, hallucinations or paranoia. Pt relates a long involved detained scenario of a "a Jewish doctor programming me to kill my catholic wife. " Pt ruminates on this though out the interview. He states his admission today was prompted by his "becoming cognitively aware of the programming in 3/81. Pt gives details of an "algorithm" to kill her – "step one was spot, step 2 was "red" and step 3 was dot. Spot is the name of a restaurant the Pres. Bush visited. Pt has a poster for Bush and Cheney which had red in it. And if Dot his wife showed up wearing red, he was to kill her. Pt states he swore to the Air Force he would never touch a weapon after he was dx'd psychotic in 1981. Pt states he was programmed by the Air Force to kill his wife and he wants

monetary compensation from the government in the amount of $3 Trillion.

Of note- the current movie "The Manchurian Candidate" is very similar to pt's delusion.

Childhood Hx: Raised in New York by both parents. He is the oldest of 4 children, and 3 younger siblings: Ellen, Douglas, and Maryann. Has contact with siblings and parents. Pt states he was constantly mentally abused by "my Nazi prick father"

Hobbies/Activities " reading especially Tom Clancy

Sexual Orientation : celibate x 6 yrs heterosexual

Religion : zen catholic

PROGRESS NOTE page 67 VAMC entry date Jan 12, 2003 Author Martin, Michael J

Vet seen at the group home. He has reported that he moved out of the group home into his own apartment. The manager of the group home has agreed to watch out for this veteran and manage his affairs. Veteran is 100% SC and affairs should be monitored by the VA. This arrangement by the manager is not recommended by this writer, unless he is registered. The group home has decided to close and Dr. Walters has said that this veteran may be ready to try and live independently. Veteran is discharged on this date. He will be welcome back into the CRC program if efforts to live on his own should fail

PROGRESS NOTE page 68 VAMC entry date Dec, 05 2002 Author Martin, Michael J

Veteran attended the thanksgiving dinner. He was dressed appropriately for the outing, he was clean and in good spirits. Vet talked about his pending move and was pleased to hear that Dr. Walters felt he was ready to try living independently.

Writer will continue to follow this vet with his transition. Vet was given my business card and told how to contact me if he needed my assistance.

PROGRESS NOTE page 68 VAMC entry date Nov 21, 2002
Author: Brown, Clarice

CRC home visit made with vet during the annual inspection of the Veteran's house, 414 South Main Ave, Sidney Ohio. Mr. Keller has been a resident of the home since 7/1/98 and was recently informed that the sponsor /Audrey Willis plans to close this CRC home 31 Dec 2002. This vet will report his alternative living arrangement with his assigned social worker, Michael Martin.

PROGRESS NOTE page 69 VAMC entry date Nov 6, 2002
Author Martin, Michael J

Vet was visited in the group home. He was in a joyous mood. He talked about playing golf. Vet said he has been doing well and he showed me a letter that he presented to the caregiver with his intension to move. Vet has showed better judgment recently and he may be ready to try living independently. Vet could be monitored for a short time. Mr. Keller has accepted an invitation to the PSR thanksgiving dinner. Vet will continue to be monitored to assist him in the decision to determine if he can live on his own.

PROGRESS NOTE page 70 VAMC entry date Oct, 11 2002
Author: Martin, Michael J

The vet was seen in the group home this date. The vet remains compliant with medication and has no complaints. He reports no S/H ideations. The veteran's affect is broad. Today, the vet was pleasant and well-groomed. Vet was alert and stated he had no problems.

Vet said he still gets visit from his sons and ex-wife. Vet said that relationship is going very well.

The vet was visited Oct 06,2002 in the group home by writer. A copy of the veteran's medications and appointments were provided to the caregiver and the vet. Vet was pleased to see me and was in a joyful mood. Vet said he enjoyed the baseball game that we attended with the CRC program Vet was dressed appropriately and very cooperative. Vet reports eating well and sleeping well. He enjoys eating out and he is able to afford that vet is able to manage his own money and he is very proud of the fact that he has not been in the hospital for 4 years. Vet is still benefiting from the CRC program and remains at the level of care.

The vet was visited July 16, 2002 in the group home where he has lived for the past 3 years. Vet remains stable and appropriately placed. Mr. Keller was in good spirits and states that he is doing well in the group home. Vet appears to be eating well and sleeping good. Vet has a private room and he follows the house rules for leaving the home by letting the caregiver know where he is going. Vet is visited by his family, sons and ex-wife, they go to dinner and he describes it as a good relationship. Vet has no complaints at this time.

November 4, 2006

PROGRESS NOTE page 78 VAMC entry date Feb 11, 2002
Author: Martin, Michael J

Writer spoke with vet by phone after caregiver informed social worker that Mr. Keller would be going on a extended vacation with his family. Vet will be gone for 6 weeks and has had problems in the past when he has gone for that length of time. Plans to have enough medication and a temporary address that medication could be sent to have been discussed and Mr. Keller said he would take care of plans to receive his medication

PROGRESS NOTE page 85 VAMC entry date June 11, 2001 Author Martin, Michael J

This veteran attended baseball game as part of group outing for CRC program. Time was spent with the vet discussing problems and concerns at the group home. No problems were reported by the patient at this time. The vet's behavior was good during the game and he socialized and mixed well with other group members.

PROGRESS NOTE page 88 VAMC entry date March 20, 2001 Author: Sehbi, Simran Kaur

Mr. Keller is a 50 – year old white male vet with a diagnosis of bipolar type 1, who was accompanied to the Mental Health Clinic by staff members from the Veterans home where he resides. Patient sees Dr. Walters, but missed last one or two appointments. " I had gone to Florida with my parents". He came today to get his medication refilled.

This 50 – year old white male vet wearing dark glasses and a hat, carrying a very professional looking bag, in which he stated he had a manuscript of a book he has been writing about himself.

PROGRESS NOTE page 121 Dayton VAMC entry date Sept 29, 1998 Author Humphrey , Donna

Home visit made on 9/22/98. Vet was very friendly, smiled easily, was getting ready to take a walk which he did after speaking with me for a short period of time. Vet reports no problems or concerns at this time. Will continue to monitor placement and provide services as needed.

Vet resides in Residential Care Home in Sidney, OH, Veteran's house. Home visit made today. Vet reports that he saw his 2 sons over the weekend continues to have frequent contact with them. He also states that he is talking with his father who lives in New York and that they are getting along well, which has never happened before. He states that he plans to fly home in July for his parents' 50th anniversary celebration and that they will be driving him home. House manager states that vet has been stable and no problems noted. Vet has done extremely well in this placement. Will continue to monitor placement.

Home visit made on 1/11/98 to veteran's group home. Vet states that he continues to like the home, that he has weekly contact with his sons, and has had several visits from them. Home reports that vet has again requested that his VA checks be sent directly to him instead of his brother, but no one knew this until 1/1/98. Mr. Keller did pay his rent and his other financial obligations with the encouragement and assistance of the home manager. He states that he feels that he is " a man" and should be able to handle his funds.

Home visit made on 11/16/98. Vet had been out for a walk when I first arrived. Reports that he is happy with the home, that the food is good. House manager states that vet receives phone call from his children every few weeks. He has also had contact with his ex-wife who did come to visit him. Family in NY continues to manage vet's funds. Goal is continued placement.

PROGESS NOTE page 127 Dayton VAMC entry date Sept 24, 1998 Author Sutherland, Janet U

Pt informed worker on Sept 16 that he would like to reach wife who continues to live in Danville, VA. Pt and his wife married at Virginia Beach, 1994. Pt is service connected, as well as his wife. He met her during their placement on psych at the Salem VA Medical Center. Pt reports he would like to reunite with her and make a go of their marriage. Worker agreed to contact Salem VA Medical Center to speak with a social worker in hope of making contact with someone who knew Mrs. Keller. Worker spoke with Debra in the social work department who knew pt's wife. She informed worker that Mr. Bill Furgerson, MSW, is the assigned worker. Worker learned that MRS. Keller was an in-pat on psych at that time. Worker left a message for social worker to return the call. Pt agreed to simply send his wife flowers for now.

PROGRESS NOTE page 131 Dayton VAMC entry August 05, 1998 Author Hugger, Raymond

Pt stopped by the unit and asked to see me. Pt. Stated he's happy with the group home he's now in, and that he likes the community (Sidney).

He added that he's been in contact with his sons, and he's set up a visit to see them soon. Money is being handled by pt's family in NY.

PROGRESS NOTE page 133 Dayton VAMC entry June 26, 1998 Author Hugger, Raymond

Pt's family in NY is willing to resume financial POA responsibility and willing to front money for a RCH placement here, but unwilling to come for pt. "until he shows he can be stable here in Ohio " Pt. Has been accepted for a Sidney RCH (VETERAN'S HOUSE) 414 S. Main, Sidney 45365; owner Audrey Willis for on or about the 1st of July. Brother Douglas will send the $1,300 rent money for July to Audrey. Bank manager at pt's bank here knows pt., and will close out pt's account when pt's address in NY. I've given John Kelley NY account info. From changing the direct deposit for August's check to NY.

PROGRESS NOTE page 134 Dayton VAMC entry June 25, 1998 Author Johnson, Dennis L

Mr. Keller has been seen daily this week. He is continuing to look stable and to discuss his plans in a rational and appropriate manner. He is scheduled to go to a group home in Sidney after the first of July. He has also agreed to arrange that his July check be sent to his mother as he is aware that his recent checks have not been used in his own best interest and that access to large sums of money has seemed to be a factor in triggering hospitalization. He verbalizes a strong desire to have continued regular contact with is 2 sons. He has discussed his relationship with his first wife (mother of his sons) and some continuing feeling of loss about the end of that relationship. He expresses willingness to participate in a day treatment program following hospitalization, which would appear to be an appropriate modality.

PROGRESS NOTE page 135 Dayton VA Medical Center June 16, 1998 Author: Johnson, Dennis

Mr. Keller was seen individually today as well as with the treatment team. We discussed what he wants to do with is life. He stated that he does not want to go back to New York; instead he would like to stay in the Fairborn area to be close to his 2 boys as he feels that this what he wants most in his life; he is willing to accept someone else having control of his money – even though he does not like it, he states that he sees it as necessary to maintain stability. He would like to return to Hope House if possible as he feels this is the best plan to allow him to maintain stability to be a good influence for his sons. He compares himself unfavorably to their step-father who is stable and doing well financially. He talks of enjoying periods of high activity and excessive spending which are followed by periods like the current one in which he is self critical. He denies being angry and resentful of others, only of himself for his bad behavior. He indicates he is staying in bed, sleeping excessively now, misses being able to go to movies and restaurants. Patient sits with slumped posture, downcast eyes, occasional smiling, prone to agree with statement and suggestions and to respond with platitudes, some restlessness, becomes more agitated when confronted. Mr. Keller , as during his last hospitalization after manic symptoms were controlled, appears rather placid, withdrawing, superficially compliant, but reluctant to actively engage in participatory problem solving. Plan continued contacts to encourage patient to explore options and actively participate in decisions about his future

PROGRESS NOTE page 137 Dayton VA Medical Center June 11, 1998 Author: Hugger, Raymond

Recent telephone and e-mail contacts with pt's brother and pt's NY case manager. Brother Douglas states pt's behavior is typical of past pattern. Bro says he's come to get pt. Before, and may be able to do so again- he wants to talk it over with family first, and adds, "I won't come for him – or speak with him by phone – until he's stable (I tried to transport him before and had him run off), and there'll have to be something firm set-up for him back in NY"

Case Manager reports that Sunken Meadows will take pt. Back – "But not on an .I.OU. - he'll need to pay his bill cash. PT has spent his benefit check for June and is broke.

PROGRESS NOTE page 140 Dayton VA Medical Center June 9, 1998 Author: Altman, Susan

PT continues to be loose. Ambulating about the unit. Singing loudly. Continues to ask for paper to write on. Signs on door stating, warning restricted area, use of deadly force, General Keller Command Control Center with a picture of a military tent.

PROGRESS NOTE page 157 Dayton VA Medical Center May 07, 1998 Author : Humphrey Donna

Received call from Mental Health Greene County, that vet was picked up by police after motel staff where vet was staying called for help after vet threatened suicide. She has been called in to evaluate. Vet gave her my name and stated that he would agree to come to VA for evaluation. Vet had received a letter from WPAFB that he was no longer allowed on base. He was noted to have written several times "death before dishonor" and when asked by Ms. Eisenhut about a method he stated that he was going to drink whiskey and take a full bottle of lithium. Notified Dennis Johnson, psychologist covering ER for psych of above situation and that vet would be brought in by police for eval.

PROGRESS NOTE page 163 Dayton VA Medical Center April 17, 1998 Author: Johnson, Dennis

Mr. Keller was interviewed with the treatment team this a.m. He was agitated and overtly very hostile toward team members especially the psychiatrist with ethic reference and references to him as a "fool". He stated that it is all becoming more clear now and made delusional references connecting events on the ward to an alleged murder a number of years ago

PROGRESS NOTE page 163 Dayton VA Medical Center April 15, 1998 Author: Hugger, Raymond

I just spoke to Sharon from HOPE house and she is willing to take Kevin back at discharge if he will agree to a payee. The problem was that when he got his money, he packed his bags and went to a local motel, then in two days he returned to the home. He did give her $500 which was half the rent. She feels that he will probably do the same thing next month. And he does still owe her for the rest of this month.

PROGRESS NOTE page 170 Dayton VA Medical Center April 3, 1998 Author: Humphrey Donna

Staff from HOPE House called to report that Mr. Keller had moved out although he stated that he liked the home, but that several Colonels…he named five…at the WPAFB told him that he would not get clearance to fly planes again as long as he lived in a Rehab Center. Home staff tried to convince him to remain in the home at least for another month since he did owe them a 30 day notice or the rent in lieu of the notice, so he paid them $500 before he left. He also told them rather loudly not to call this writer to try to convince him to stay as "I had no right to tell him what to do" He indicated when he left that he would return to get his medications, but has not yet done this. Staff reports that he was somewhat agitated and rather loud and hyper during this time. He stated that he would be staying at the Falcon Motel which is near the home.

Staff from the home confirmed that he is at this time staying at the motel. I will follow up with this by 4/8/98 by paying a visit to the motel to discuss the situation with him if possible

PROGRESS NOTE page 170 Dayton VA Medical Center March 23, 1998

Mr. Keller was transported to HOPE house, 201 W. Dayton Dr, Fairborn, OH 45324 on 3/17. HOPE House was chosen at this home is close to his sons, who live in Beavercreek, and also had a private room available. He had not previously toured the home but states after he got to the home and looked around that he was very pleased with it, that his previous group home in New York was not nearly as nice. Mr. Keller signed the appropriate paperwork regarding placement and was provided with a copy of resident's rights. Will monitor placement with weekly contact with the home and month visits to the veteran.

PROGRESS NOTE page 185 Dayton VA Medical Center June 8, 1992 Author: Harrison, Bruce

Mr. Kevin J Keller took a regular discharge from the Dom on 6/2/92. Conferral with the Cleveland VARO indicated that they had received his application for the Chapter 31 voc. Rehab. Program. Since Mr. Keller left no phone number at which to contact him. He will be discontinued for current voc. rehab. Until he initiates contact with Psychology Service.

PROGRESS NOTE page 187 Dayton VA Medical Center April 27, 1992 Author: Harrison, Bruce

Mr. Kevin J Keller is 100% SC for manic-depressive reaction, and is currently being treated with Lithium and Tegretol. In the past he tended to discontinue his medication when he felt better, with the result that his functioning periodically would deteriorate for an extended amount of time. He has been service-connected since 1981, but functioned fairly well until he was divorced in 1987. He now understands that it is important that he continue with his medication if he is to maintain his stability.

Mr. Keller obtained a B.S. in Industrial Technology in 1981, and was employed as a computer technician (repairing computers and installing hardware and software) from 11/84 to 6/87 until he was laid off in a RIF. His next two jobs were placements through a temporary technical manpower firm. The first involved data entry for a project which lasted from 10/88 to 1/89. His last employment was as a bagger at an Air Force commissary from 1/90 to 3/92.

Mr. Keller has two sons from his former marriage who live in the Dayton area. He personally has no local residence, but does have an address P.O. Box 1293, Fairborn, Ohio 45324. He is nearing the end of his S-1 stay, and is to be screened for the Dom tomorrow.

Mr. Keller will be applying for the Chapter 31 voc. rehab,

program for SC veterans, and would appear to have sufficient occupational handicap to be accepted into the program.

PROGRESS NOTE page 188 Dayton VA Medical Center April 19, 1992 Author: Flamer, Barbara

Vet has been in and out of bed most of this tour. He stated that he would like to relocate to the Dayton area and become reacquainted with his children. Vet also states that he has been in heartbreaking relationships and that is why he is here. Client says that he needs to be redirected from the wrong type of woman. Mr. Keller stated that he is writing an autobiography for his children.

PROGRESS NOTE page 190 Dayton VA Medical Center April 17, 1992 Author: Baer, Nina

Subjective
Admitted because of depressive and manic phase
Objective
PT is a 41 year old white male first admission this VA. Has spent 92 days in jail due to a misunderstanding with his girlfriend. Became manic while in jail. PT states he was placed in seclusion which made him worst. Denies A/V hallucinations. Did admit to being suicidal during his jail time. But had no plans. Has 2 sons in the Dayton area. Denies use of drugs. Pleasant cooperative.

BOOK THREE

CHAPTER ONE

17 NOVEMBER 2006

I recall sleeping outdoors in an army mountain sleeping bag in 12 degrees in order to see my sons.

28 NOVEMBER 06

I have been going to Confession every Saturday and Mass every Sunday. I miss my sons. I had a wonderful confession last week. The priests at Holy Angels are such a joy to me. I talked to Belona last night on the phone. Social Security Disability is 90-120 days away.

1 JAN 2007

I have made a fool of myself in this town. Very manic. I am a jerk sometimes. Had to call Jack on the car. I blew my money. Someday I will learn. Christmas and New Years ok. I miss my sons. Depressive.

7 JAN 2007

It is horrid what Lonnie did to my sister, Maryann. He took the house and the kids and used the courts to crush her. What is wrong with this country that uses Law to crush marriage and family. I am fed up. There is no family or faith in this country but the dollar bill. It's just plain wrong and the good people like my sister are the ones hurt. If you have money you have it all.

15 JAN 2007

My life is a mess. I have hurt my sons. I have hurt Dorothy.

Why do I yell? Depressive. I am sad. I get along with my father. He has caused me much pain. I have hurt my sons out of this pain. Oh well the bills are getting paid and I've got food to eat. Theresa is handling the bills very well. Got a Christmas gift from Belona. I have stopped blowing money. This is good.

16 Jan 2007

Had dream. I was in prison. I was hit with black baton. David as child came running down hall followed by Dorothy. Dorothy and I walked into park and we were back together. It was a delightful dream.

17 January 2007

I had dream. I was secret agent. Washington destroyed. I uncovered the plot. Lots of press. Dad looking on in the crowd. I was a hero. I love that dream. I want to be a hero. I want attention. I want my father to love me. My suit was cool at the press release.

24 January 2007

I hate lithium so much I went off it again in Dec and again in January and now I cannot sleep. So I am back on with Theresa watching me pack the pill box. I hate the tremors in my hands from lithium. OH well Kevin that's the breaks. I email Belona all the time. She is a very pretty girl. Cebu girls are very sweet. There is news that social security will arrive soon. That will be nice. I am disabled but never filed with social security but they tell me I did. I'm half crazy so we will see what happens. Fact is I don't know what I am doing half the time.

25 January 2007

Dr Phil's book on "Self Matters" is very good. I am living in the past. I am living a "fictional self". Really good book on turning your life around and living the cool life you want. Therapy good today and Theresa came with me. It's so true that I live in the past. I've got 35 years left to get it right. I am going to read Dr Phil's book cover to cover. Back on lithium and sleep is slowly getting better. It's hard to admit that most of my life is a lie. I have been a liar and master manipulator. I don't like me but the show is not over and I've got another 35 yrs to get it right. My sons are right in being mad. I'm far from a good father. Sad and depressed doesn't cut it anymore. I'm quite glad for this book that seems written for me. I lost my dream a long ,long time ago. I wear the Cebu shirts that Belona sent for Christmas. This month I am in the black. Thank God for that. This Sunday Theresa and I go to China Garden for our dinner together. 2 yrs of friendship. This book is full of good stuff that I need to hear. Basically I must change my life and live a life full of color and joy once again. There is no reason I can't do this.

26 JANUARY 2007

I am abusive towards women. I yelled at Dot. Married Yvonne for her money. Yelled at Theresa. I am not such a nice guy. I have learned to be my father. I yelled at my sons. This is sad. Douglas emailed me today about my behavior. He is right. The abuse must stop. Sunday is the China Garden with Theresa. Her birthday is February.

5 FEBRUARY 2007

Still have not heard from Dan and Dave. This is quite sad.. I think about them all the time. I am just wasting my time. My life is about me. I can't do anything about the past.

14 March 2007

Dan wrote me. We are emailing. Life is delightful

28 April 2007

Dad died 20 March. I had no clue who that was in the coffin. It certainly didn't look like Dad. The wake was quite weird. All these people that I hadn't seen since childhood. So I just would hang out and pretend this whole thing wasn't happening. Back at Levittown, New York with Mom and Maryann things weren't any better. Mom was so angry at everything. Maryann just slept all day and night. The dog barked all night and kept me up. Things were just delightful. I had no idea that Mom drank so much white wine. My family is very dysfunctional. My father was no happy camper. He wanted to die and got his wish. One day out of the blue he told Mom he was going to die. He laid foam cushions on the couch and lay there and only drank milk and ice water. Next thing, he told Mom to bring him to the hospital. He was dead in two days. What upset everyone the most was went they put him on life support. All those tubes in his body really freaked Mom out. I hadn't seen Dad in over a year and a half. He had lost so much weight that he didn't look like Dad at all. At the funeral home they had to tell me that that was Dad. This is not going to happen to me. Dad lost his enjoyment in life when he lost his eyesight. He just gave up. However, diabetes took his eyesight when he didn't stay on top of it. This is not going to happen to me. NO way. If you want a quality life, you have to work at it. Just because my family is dysfunctional doesn't mean that I have to be. I am not going to skip my meds but I have not taken lithium because it is just too toxic and is affecting my nervous system. Sometimes my hands shake so bad that I can't write or hold a coffee cup. I have Bi-Polar friends that have found less toxic meds than lithium.

30 April 2007

Sidney is so delightful after over a month in New York. At the "Alcove" I saw old friends. I have decided to do something to better my health. I am walking everywhere. I am eating smaller portions, and eating right. I am not going to settle for my old life of lying around feeling sorry for myself. I am going to get in shape and make the most of my life. Theresa is so very good for me. She really is a great help. Today we walked to the stores after coffee on our 3rd floor porch over looking the grounds. Life is awesome.

1 May 2007

Well my exercise program is going great. Theresa and I walked to the China Garden Buffet and pigged out. Oh well, nobody is perfect. The house is in order and everything is in its place thanks to Theresa. Stable life has never been my strong point, but as normal may be boring, a healthy lifestyle has a lot to offer me.

3 May 2007

I am paying bills on time, and it feels great. God, do I like spending money. It seems that I am not happy until I am blowing every dime I have, but things do change. Paying bills is just one way that I can show that I am improving. I also love wearing clean clothes. This is good. Over all things are looking up. I did the food shopping at Sidney Food Town, and I do enjoy that. Theresa is at Kroger and walked all the way there, some 7 miles. Well maybe someday I will be able to do that. Meanwhile I will enjoy drinking my coffee on the 3rd floor porch. No more negative balance in my bank statements. Gee this feels great

5 MAY 2007

As I reflect on the past, I remember walking the streets of Danville, Virginia late at night looking for my second wife Yvonne. Some kids in a passing car came up at me from my back and hit me hard pushing me towards the bridge. God saved me by allowing me to hit the guard rails and not to fall off the bridge.. Later that night the cops picked me up off the street and I next was to lie on the cement floor of a jail cell. My back hurt bad. As I watched TV of a 50's dance I cried. What a life I've had. But now I live in a nice apartment with Theresa my God-send. The streets are cruel. I don't remember how I did arrive homeless in Dayton. I stayed at St. Vincent's in the evening and had to leave early in the morning. I spent a lot of time at the Dayton Library. Everything I owned had to be carried all around the streets. You never get used to the streets. I forget a lot of the emotional pain. I am focusing on now. Today I had wanted to go to confession with Fr Jerry. God has been good to me. God got me off the streets and into this wonderful apartment with my best friend Theresa

9 MAY 2007

The construction work at the Towne Centre   Apartments continues. The second complex is just about finished. I reflect upon sleeping in a tent at the family camping area of Wright-Patt AFB. I was a sad and lonely person back then. All my possessions were in that tent. After my divorce from Dot I just gave up. I was depressed for years. Once in 12 degrees I slept in an army mountain sleeping bag in the woods to be close to my sons. Sometimes sleeping in the men's room at the Air Force Base. Living a stable life is hard to adjust too. Clean clothes are very nice after years of not having them. It's hard to find a washer and dryer when you're homeless and out of money because you're too sick to control it. Theresa is my God-send. All I have is due to her. God, have I come a long way from the "Thorazine Kid" playing ping-pong with a yellow ping-pong ball on a VA psych ward back in the 1980's. God is good. Praise God!!! Solar Systems is installing my new 3.4 gigahertz dual core system unit in June 07. This is going to be cool. I can't wait for this. Christmas in June. Tharon vows it will be a SWEET system. After 8 years with this boat anchor that pretends to be a computer, this will be a novel surprise. I am also enjoying my Motorola Razr cell phone. I am taking photos of everything. I really enjoy this Razr cell phone.

11 MAY 2007

God is good. Solar Systems installs the new 3.4 Gigahertz system unit next week. Fighting with this boat anchor is trying my stress factors. Tharon, from Solar is really cool. I am so happy. We will next start to upgrade the apartment with new furniture. Life is good. Now if only I could lose 30 pounds, that would be really cool. Oh, well some things take time. This beats a psych ward any day. Sometimes I wonder what my life would have been like if Dot didn't divorce me. Well, that's over and done with. Can't change the past. Just learn from it I guess.

Construction continues at the apartment complex. The second apartment building is almost done. I hope the pool goes in next. They say it will be in by the summer. Man, will that be sweet. All my life I have craved attention. I suppose to gain my father's who was never there.

Hopefully my sons and I will play golf this year. Just to own a car will be a big step. It's been at least 10 yrs since I've had a car. Up until now my life has been a train wreck. Always on the road, and the streets. Con man and poet and saint. I don't know why my life has been so dysfunctional. I now enjoy a stable life. It is boring but the rewards offer a good return. What does it matter by which name we call God. Allah, Yahweh, or Christ. What is in a name?? Is not the soul and spiritual wonder of our being the primal issue? Somehow years ago I was living in City Parks in the forest. Now I enjoy a wonderful new apartment. How did this happen? Answer: God. God is God. Does it really matter what name we call Him? The native Indian called God the "Great Spirit" and at wounded Knee our US Army killed unarmed men, women and children. Delightful. Why does man love to kill? Time is marked in hours, minutes, and seconds. Yet we go to a place of no time. When my sons were born I knew that there must be a God. How else explain the birth of your sons? We are here just passing travelers. This is not our home. My flesh shall rot. It shall feed the earth. The living bio-mass we call "Mother Earth" shall go on. In the remaining 35 yrs or so, I shall develop my interest in photos, and computer technology, and drama. I shall find me. The person that God the Father created. God is good. Life is good. Praise God! I exist in order to tell the tale of God's awesome creation called life. Why some would choose death I have no concept of. To kill babies just is so horrid that I can't comment on it. The excuses for this fall short of the glory of God. To self-destruct is evil. God chose life for his creation. For man to take it away is wicked, and evil. I must be mad to actually say this in print. It is not politically correct. How sad of this generation. We live for self. But self is but an illusion. This July, I will have been here in Sidney 9 years. I have no idea where the time has gone. On Saturday I will see Fr Jerry for confession. Best part of my day. Fr Jerry is totally cool. I just love confession, and always have. It's psychotherapy to me. This Oct Theresa and I will get formally engaged which is a good thing. I just must settle down. I have no idea if this journal will sell. Selling the journal is not primal. It's the writing of it that is the good part for me.. Well, dinner on the table now, I'll be back later to write some more. God is good. Life is good

12 MAY 2007

Dear Dad,
I know you're dead. You died 20 March 07. Somehow it doesn't seem real. I don't know where you are. You were very hard on me as a teen and young man. I hated your guts. You were always working. I never saw you. I resented you and how you treated me. You were always putting me down. I hated that. Now you're dead. I miss you in some strange way. I am glad we seemed to get along in the last few years before your death. I found myself yelling at my sons the way you yelled at me. I put a stop to that. Two things stand out that bother me. First, you picked a fight with me over the unwed mother of my daughter by her. That fight was mean and cruel, totally unjust. Second, when my article in the local paper came out you told me that your eyesight prevented you from reading it. Bullshit. Oh, well I forgive you. You're dead and life goes on.

13 MAY 2007

Confession was awesome. Today I go to Mass at 10:30am. I reflect upon my face in mirror. My hair is thinning, I am getting older. I am not the handsome man I was years ago.. Life goes on. I retire to take a nap.

15 MAY 2007

The fights with "Susan" were horrid. We fought all the time. Her jealousy was unreal. We met at a bus stop. Her cute dress and pretty face and pink socks won me over. When she got off the bus I never thought I would see her again. She called me that night with the phone number I gave her. I was staying on Base. We had a delightful dinner, and drove around, and one thing led to another and she invited me to her beautiful apartment. Sex on the first date was awesome. What I didn't realize was that I was caught in her web now. The fights over stupid stuff just got worse and worse. One fight involved throwing things around in her apartment till we broke her storm door. Glass was everywhere. The kitchen was full of broken coffee cups and plates. When she bore her first child she told me it was mine. It was not but I didn't know that then. I stayed with her till she burnt my home trailer to the ground in 1993. I knew then I would have to ditch the bitch. Her second child was born August 1993 and this little girl was mine; however I didn't believe her till the blood tests were in. This little girl was so pretty and cute. To be honest I was not there when she was born. I was busy flirting with someone else. There are many things I wish I could redo. That is one of them. Then came the day I found out she was married to a guy overseas in the Army. Now things really heated up. Her husband serving his country deserved much better than this. So, that was that. When I got my next check I hopped a greyhound to Dayton, Ohio to be with my sons. "Susan's" husband was willing to work things out even with a child not his. She left him to track me down in Dayton. I was inpatient at the Dayton VA Medical Center and she came to visit me and after the visit broke through the electronic doors to come on the psych ward after visitation hours. I was shocked to learn she had one of my VA checks in her pocketbook. She even tried to have me sign her brother's government check; if I had, I would be in jail now. She was just amazing. She would do anything for payback. The last time I saw her we were both in jail over our fights. Delightful. Well I'm tired and it's 3:37am. I'll chat more later. I am so compulsive that I cannot enjoy the "now". This is quite stupid. However, I am getting better. The new 3.4 gigahertz dual core system is coming next week. That will be so cool. I have no idea where my daughter is or what she looks like. This is sad. Hope that her adoptive family is treating her well. Oh well. There is nothing that I can do about this. Nightmares last night. No idea why I get them. Will buy a digital cam soon.

16 MAY 2007

Theresa and I go to Aspen Wellness Center today to see Mercedes. They are very good to us. We will talk about money. I feel at 56 I must learn how to handle money. Hiding the cards from me is stupid. This is not the solution. Just got back from Aspen and got my checkbook and credit cards from Theresa. Every week Theresa and I will go over what I am spending on the credit cards. The outcome of all this is that I feel more in control of my money. Mercedes is just great. She is quite professional as is the staff of Aspen. I am lucky to have them.

Just got an email from my son Dan. God, it feels great to hear from him. We still don't have a date to get together but his kind words meant a lot to me. Maybe I can be a good father in the 35 yrs or so I have left. The 3.4 gigahertz system is coming next week. That is way cool. I will try to budget for uploading this ebook to the editor in July 07 my father's birthday month. It's 8pm. Theresa made an awesome meal as usual. My life is now stable. What will I do when this ebook is uploaded to the editor at iuniverse? Mercedes told me today that my writing shows talent. That made me feel really good. I can actually do something. How delightful. I am not overmedicated anymore. I cut the valproic acid in half. I cut the lithium by 2 pills a day. I feel fine. I am sleeping well. God is good. Life is good.

17 MAY 2007

It's 1:00am and I had a dream that my father was alive. Man, was that strange. In this dream he is in his room again. He turned to see me. Reality has sunk in that I will never see him again. I do hope he is happy in his afterlife. He looked so weird last time I saw him in that coffin. Well, it's time to go back to bed. Will chat latter. God is good. Life is good. It's 2:00pm and I did go back to sleep. As I reflect upon my past I remember the beautiful townhouse that Dorothy and I owned. I am now left with a starter apartment with a collection of odd furnishings. That's the nature of divorce. Maryann my sister is really getting the royal shaft. It's just so sad what we do to each other here in America where everyone wants to be rich. Marriage seems to be of so little value here. It's now 7:00pm, and dinner was great. I seem to have many dreams on jail. I think my time in jail has had an impact on me. I really did not belong there however many others have fared much worst than I.

And I have much to thank God for. Theresa has been a very good friend. I will have to take her out to dinner or something. I really can't help anyone but myself. Art, to me, is picking up the broken parts of your life and creating Art for Art's sake. Will chat latter. God is good. Life is good.

18 MAY 2007

Theresa is walking to Big Lots today. I have no idea how she walks 7 miles. I can't do it. I am not in shape like I once was in the Air Force.

Much has changed since the Elite Guard at Scott Air Force Base. Somehow I must be content in the "now". This surely beats sleeping in the tent at family campground at Wright-Patt. Stability has its rewards. "Papajohn's " is on the way. How bad can this life be? Parts being ordered by Solar Systems next week. What do I have to complain about? Does stability get any better than this? No, I don't make the money to have everything I want but that's just a part of life. Do you ever have enough money? I now fancy myself as a writer. This I can do. The ebook may not sell but writing this is emotionally healing. As I reflect, I recall Danville Virginia and my attempt to find my wife Yvonne. I ran out of money and was forced to stay at a church shelter. A very kind older gentleman paid for my bus fare home. Thank you Lord for such kind Christians out there. He never got paid back. I don't even remember his name. The psych nursing staff at Dayton Medical Center have also been so kind to me. Dr Walters, my shrink, has always treated me with respect and kindness. I believe in the basic goodness of man much as St Francis did. I understand the times of today with fraud, and hate, and war. That all in all does not change my respect for the basic goodness of man. So many have helped me overcome my disorder. This is why God is good and life is good. Someday I will die to meet my God. I also recall a moment in jail when we all started to sing and dance and the turnkey shouted "hey, what do you think this is: church?"

Man was born into original sin. His life is the quest to prepare himself for the afterlife. As a progressive Roman Catholic everything I see around me points to this. My confessor tells me that my sins have been confessed and therefore not to be worried about anymore. I love Holy Angels because confession is truly psychotherapy for me. The point of all this comes now to the fact that if you're Catholic you should be the best Catholic you can be and if you are Protestant you should be the best Protestant you can be. Catholics profess Christ on the Cross and Protestants profess Christ resurrected. The focus is different but we need the awareness of both. Since Christians, Jews, and Muslims profess one God, why they are killing each other is beyond me. Does it matter what we name God? God is God. His salvation exists for all mankind.

What is to happen to those who worship many Gods is not my problem. That is up to God the Father to figure out. Is there not already many factors to divide us? Why should we fight about spirituality? Isn't God big enough to be seen in many forms of awareness? The native Indian worshiped the Great Spirit yet this did not stop the US Army from killing men, women and children at Wounded Knee when they were not armed and living on their reservation. When will man stop the art of killing man? Most likely never. All of this is not my problem. My life script is one of loving my sons. That's my job in this life. It's 5:15pm and I've scanned some photos for my sons. This year I will have a car. What will that event be like??? Actually be able to drive to where I want to go. Man, will that be cool. Did I mention that my ebook will be uploaded to the editor in July 07?? Is it me or don't I have a lot to be thankful for? Well I will watch a DVD. Will chat later. God is good. Life is good

19 MAY 2007

This stupid old system can't handle video or audio. However the new system will be here soon. I installed service pack 4 on the old operating system. We will see if that helps. Recalling the stupid fight I had with the late Dorothy Whidden, my former mother-in-law. How much a jerk am I for not settling that before she died. Oh well, what is done is done. Just got back from steak and eggs at the "Alcove". It's a great breakfast. Can't find the style of café in New York. No way. Everyone knows everyone here. Maybe that's good or maybe not. I don't know. I get attention here. I like that. Well, it's 10:12 am and I got up at 4:00am. I'm going back to bed and get some sleep. It's now 6:15 pm and I'm back from Lee's Chinese. The asparagus triple delight was just wonderful. God, I love to eat. But eating all the time will kill me. I must somehow diet to a healthy eating habit. Why on earth I get up sometimes at 4:00 am , is beyond me. My body is not as strong as it once was.

Some stupid virus is slowing this system down with its sickness and killing my programs. It's amazing to me how I put up with this for so long.

Well, this old system like me is outdated. Security systems on credit cards and programs are getting to be a pain in the ass. How are we to remember all the pass codes? Maybe my mother has the right idea, for she doesn't even have an ATM card. I am not a businessman, I am a artist. Therein lies the difference between me and my brother Doug. I believe in the Art of the Word. I am a dreamer like John Lennon. Yes, at one time on the campgrounds at Wright-Patt AFB I even thought I was St. John the Baptist. Thank God, those delusions are now over. I have lost many material goods over the last 20 years. However my soul is intact. Confession was awesome today. Priests can have such kind words, it's such a shame that the bad ones are making the news all the time with sexual abuse claims arising all the time. These are indeed hard times for the just and true. I have come to doubt that peace will ever gain over war and death. Everyday in the news are more and more of our troops getting killed for their country. How sad it is that these young men getting paid so little are giving up their souls for our freedom. I owe much to the Air Force that has provided so much for me. I think perhaps that next month I will bleed a little and get this ebook to the editor and be finally done with it. So I put the bills on hold for a month to provide for this ebook to see the editor and start the process of publishing. This final event is so way overdue. I want this work in print. God is good. Life is good.. I reflect upon grandma's house that I was gifted to stay overnight in once in a while; I loved the sound of the bullfrogs in the pond at night. Those were the days of German bread cooked fresh from the bakery and lean roast beef and blueberry pies. Oh how I long for those days now gone. And how do I thank that retired Air Force Colonel, who rented me such a nice apartment right next to the San Antonio VA Medical Center? He was so kind to me. In my grandmother's basement I wrote my poetry book on loose-leaf paper. Maybe all my life I have wanted to write. Something left behind after I die. Something to pass on to the family. This ebook will not sell. I doubt it. Not enough sex and action. Nobody gets shot in these pages. Sex and murder, now that sells. Perhaps my grassroots Sidney appeal might help. Sidney does have a lot to offer that big cities like Levittown do not. The waitresses notice me here. They enjoy my generosity. At 56 I am not dead yet. I will enjoy my remaining 35 or more years. I will live for my family. It's almost 11:00pm and I will have to chat more later. Good night my friend. God is good. Life is good.

20 May 2007

Dear Silver Fox

It's 12:34 am and I can't sleep. I took 2 lithium. I recall your presence at Holy Family Church in the voice of the seagulls on the parking lot. You have been with me all my life. You saved my life when I was kidnapped by that nut case with the baseball bat in his backseat and his $5.00 offer to touch his penis after he unzipped his pants. You were there and told my mind to drive into the snow bank once I threw the door open on that car at 25 mph. You were there that day when that nice old lady invited me into her house and fed me milk and cookies and called the cops knowing something had happened. You were there with me on the streets of Dayton and Mexico. You have protected me all my life. Thank you Silver Fox for being what you are: God. I see you, Silver Fox, in the tree, and birds, and flowers, and squirrels. I will praise you and your creation all my remaining years, Silver Fox. The day my sons were born you were there, Silver Fox. Your wisdom invades the minds of men. You take them down many winding roads to test their spirit. .You, Silver Fox, are the Alpha and Omega . All life comes to you and all life will be judged by you. There is no way of getting one over on the Silver Fox. You know the ways of man. You created him in your image. Today is Sunday and I will worship you at Mass. This is only right. It is my thanksgiving for all you have done for me. God Bless God. There is only one faith and that is God. God is God. I live to write of your awesome glory. God is good. Life is good. I must try to get more sleep. Will chat more later. It's now 8:04 am Silver Fox and I sleep restless but did indeed sleep. Today is your day. I will go to Mass. I will wear my Father's Sport Coat and pray for his soul. I will pray. As I recall the psych ward at Washington D.C. I had a pass for the day. I traveled off base to the downtown area. I had a grand Chinese lunch. As I was passing though I had a panic attack. It was late and getting dark. I could not find a taxi and I wished not to arrive late at the psych ward and lose my level 4. I prayed to you, Silver Fox, and a taxi came out of nowhere. I got back 5 minutes early. No, I do not believe in Luck. I believe in God 's blessing. It is now 9:52 am and I must get some rest. It was a restless night.

The last few nights we have been watching DVDs. "Master and Commander" was good. "I, Robot was good". "War of the Worlds" with Tom Cruise was good. The visual effects of these movies are awesome. Tonight is pork chops and I am very hungry. It's a quiet Sunday. A good day for DVDs. Why I am still here is all about God. I used to have the self-destructive habit of walking dark streets at night in traffic. One time late at night I was wearing sunglasses on a street in Virginia and a truck van came within inches of hitting me. So many times I did the stupidest things. I rarely go out at night now. I have grown safety-conscienous in my latter years. Psych wards weren't always a bad trip. At Albany VA Medical Center the psych nurse took some of us to a folk music festival. It was totally cool. All I can say now is that I enjoy the comfortable living of my apartment and writing of my manic past. I am going to let my dinner digest. Will chat later. God is good. Life is good.

I was last inpatient January 2005 at Northport VA Medical Center. My male nurse was amazing. He really was a blessing when I was having a bad trip with my emotions. He was one of many that have been so kind to me. This all points to the basic goodness of man.

22 May 2007

I had a dream of Grandma last night. We were in a school that was turned into a nursing home. The whole thing was weird. It's 2:20pm and soon it will be time to go to the stores for more iced tea. I am avoiding colas. Bad for the teeth. I am trying to improve my overall health care.

Belona called today. She is so cute. Her oldest daughter is now in High School. I just don't know where the time goes. At 56 I am not at all in shape. I must do something about that if I desire to live to be 100 yrs old. It's 6:34 pm and I must let my dinner digest. Will chat more later.

Dearest Dad,
It has been a little over two months since your death on the 20th of March this year. You were very hard on me yet I think of the good times that may have been rare but in your twisted way, you did love me. I miss those good times and wish there would have been more. The back cover of this book will have that nice photo of our golf outing together. I love that photo. It is so warm and affectionate. I hope you're happy were you are. I know you were not happy here. I don't intend on going out like you. I will enjoy my life. I will enjoy my family. You wished to die and got your dream. You died quick. Somehow you planned the whole thing. Yet, after spending a lot of money on a trust fund you died without signing it.

Your temper is famous. You loved to work hard and at one time worked 3 jobs to get the things in life that you wanted. You even turned on your favorite son Douglas. Your email was horrid. I will pray for you and hope where you are now is a happy place for you. Does heaven have an email address? Let me know and I'll send you a happy and nice one to put a smile on your face. I mean 2 years ago when you broke down on the phone and kept repeating "Kevin, I love you" deserves a nice happy and loving email? Don't you think?

23 MAY 2007

Dearest Dan and Dave,

I miss you guys so much. Do you think when I get a car we could play golf? I hope so. It's been a year and a half since I've seen you. That's too long. I hope to have a car by October, my birthday month. Don't let me go to the Philippines. It's just not a good idea. I wish to devote my time too you. You are my sons. I spent a lifetime running away. Now, I stop running. Somehow I must pick up the broken parts of my life and patch them up. Somehow I must learn the art of fatherhood. I love you and always will love you. You are my sons. I wish to learn the art of fatherhood. You deserve that much. Don't you think? It's time to check the mail. God Bless. Love, your dad.

Dear Theresa,

For over 2 years now you have helped stabilize my emotions. You cook, clean, wash, and do food shopping. You provide a warm and affectionate friendship. My life has vastly improved because of your care. I have no idea where I would be today without you. I only hope our friendship grows deeper in the years to come. I thank you for being you. Your intellect is awesome. I wonder how you have retained all your insight and knowledge. Thank you so much for your love, affection, and warmth. Thank you for editing this text.

God Bless, Kevin

24 May 2007

Dear Dot,

I just wanted to tell you that you were a delightful wife and I am very sorry for the hell I put you though. I was a jerk and a flirt. You did your best but my illness did you in. I maxed out the credit cards and was a poor husband as well as father. If all this wasn't bad enough I made a scene back in 2004 that I'm sure upset you. You have been a loyal friend since 4th grade and a wonderful Mother of my 2 sons Dan, and Dave. I am very sorry things didn't work out but you did your very best. I know you don't want to hear from me but this letter is my way of expressing my emotions on the subject. We will always have Dan and Dave in common. I only pray that someday we can be friends again. Theresa treats me very well and I am sure you would approve of her. She has high morals and like you is very smart. I know that I have put you though a lot and I only hope time will heal the wounds that I have caused with my emotional outbursts. Oh well, time moves on. I was just wondering if you remembered walking in the snow on Southern State Parkway and climbing trees together?. Do you remember Holy Family School? You were always smart. Do you remember Binghamton, New York? Well, I only wish you the very best. Thanks for the great job you did with Dan and Dave. They are the best reflection of you. I admit I was a big flirt and you did not deserve that but I never did cheat on you. I guess all that is water over the dam now. I do miss you and our family lunch together at Lee's Chinese. You're a very good ex-wife and I am sorry that I blew it. Thank you also for that very first steak dinner you made for me at your Mom's house. I guess I was 17 years old. You were a big part of my youth. I do hope someday you will forgive me for all the emotional upset I have caused you. I have not made your life easy, have I? God Bless You!!!

25 May 2007

Just woke up from a dream in which dad was knocking on his coffin lid because he was alive. Horrid dream. I am buying a used car from Jack. I want to drive to Fairborn to see my sons. It has been over a year and a half. We will meet at the "Flying Tiger". I do hope they can fit me in. I am also taking the written exam for my license today. That has been put off for a year. I must get my license. I am 56 years old and tired of walking for 8 years. Passed the written exam with a 83. Road test 7 June 11:30. I am getting the auto from Superior Auto. Soon I will be driving my own car. I can't believe it.

26 May 2007

Breakfast at the "Alcove" was great. Steak and Eggs. Credit cards maxed out again. This has got to stop. Gave my checkbook and credit cards back to Theresa. Someday I will learn the art of money. I don't know why I overdosed in late 1995. I took a whole bottle of Fentanyl and followed it with a whole bottle of Jack Daniels. I got into my car and raced down the highway and passed out at the wheel. The Ohio State Highway Police got me out of the car and transported me to the nearest hospital where my stomach was pumped with activated charcoal. These men in blue saved my life.

27 May 2007

Pentecost Sunday

Thank you Lord for your indwelling spirit. Make me a vessel of your fire. Help me to love Theresa as she is: the best friend that I have ever had. Together we edit the manuscript. She copyedits the ebook. We work well as a team. It is providential.

30 May 2007

Theresa has finished copyediting the journal so far. I will pay for food June and July and start paying her back for food expenses.

31 May 2007

Friday Solar Systems delivers the new 3.4 gig hertz duo core system unit. The customer service of Solar Systems is outstanding. I am very pleased to do business with them. Friday I get my new car. I have been without a car for over 8 years. Superior Auto has been very helpful. More dreams of Dorothy and "Cris" last night. I've come a long way from writing poems in grandma's basement. This has been a lazy day. Not much going on. Waiting for the big day on Friday. God, a new car and a new computer all in one day. It will be a grand day for me.

Tonight Theresa made a delightful dinner. I just know if I put my mind to it, I can stick to a budget. At 56 yrs old it's about time that I do so.

Friday is payday so it's a good time for fiscal common sense. I want to make Theresa happy.

Dear Dad,
I miss you. Next month is your birthday month. I only wish now that you have passed away we would have done more things together.

I am glad for the good times we had sharing our love for Tom Clancy novels. As for the hard times they are done and over. I found in my garage the basket of golf balls you sent me with the words "have a ball with golf" I will enjoy golf thinking of you looking down from heaven at me. I know you last days were hard on you after losing your vision. I am taking care of my high blood sugar. God bless you Dad. Rest in peace. Love Kevin your Son

1 JUNE 2007

The new system unit from solar systems is awesome. This thing is smoking. Very very fast. Picked up new car today. Great day for me. Theresa was good about the added expense. She is a doll.

3 JUNE 2007

With new car and new computer budget tight. Like a jerk I must have left on the lights. Battery dead today. Jack is going to check it out on Tuesday. Audrey came over and we all went over to Kroger's. I drove. I loved it. Haven't seen my sons in over a year. Hope to see them soon. They are very busy with school and jobs. It's going to be a few month's before iuniverse gets this journal. The budget is too tight right now. I am getting killed with cash advance fee's. The compulsive spending is costing me. Somehow I must gain control of this issue. Oh well, this is nothing new. We all have issues. My issue is spending. Kroger was good today. Free food. Never see that at Food Town. It is lightening outside but I am not going to unplug this system a third time. The storm will pass. If the battery is going to be any kind of problem, it's going to be replaced. I am not going to the Dayton VA Medical Center without a good working car. The wireless keyboard and mouse are cool with the new system unit. Usual people on the internet begging for money. I am not a bank that is for sure.

4 JUNE 2007

The budget is tight and Theresa is not getting paid back all the money I owe her for food. She is of course upset. I just must pay her back and make small payments on the credit cards. This is only fair. It was my decision to go into debt. Theresa hates debt and rightly so. I guess I love debt because I am always bouncing in and out of it. Well, if I can do this debt thing then I can undo this debt thing. Getting this journal published with have to wait till the money is right.. Something must be done about my compulsive spending habits. Oh I just love spending money, especially when I don't have it to spend. Theresa is much more conservative about money. She is wise and I am not. She watches the numbers and I do not. There is no reason that I can't learn this behavior. I am creating pain. Now, I have a tight budget to live with. I surely must not make it worst instead of better.

5 JUNE 2007

The driving lesson going very well. I am still nervous. More dreams of jail at night. Another driving lesson on Wednesday. Theresa cooks, cleans, and washes clothes. I am very happy. Tharon at Solar Systems is delightful and very helpful. Just got off the phone with my sister Maryann. She is really going through a tough time. She is very depressed. She hasn't seen her kids in over a year. Theresa is walking out to Wal-Mart. I hope all goes well on Thursday because I really want my driver's license. It's 8:24pm and Theresa is not home yet. I miss her when she is not around. Her dinner's are out of this world. She has talent. Well. it's 10:48 time to go to bed

6 JUNE 2007

More dreams of jail. This is odd. I'm up early and wish to go back to bed. I am now living with the result of maxing out 3 credit cards. How do I do this? Why, do I mishandle money like this? Today another driving lesson. I do hope I pass the exam on Thursday. I wish to drive.

8 June 2007

I passed my road test. I drove food shopping and to the golf range. I will master the fundamentals of the golf swing.

9 June 2007

I like yahoo better than Microsoft for messenger and other stuff. Well it's time to write my sons another letter.

30 July 2007

IT HAS BEEN MY HONOR TO BE INVITED INTO THE ELVIS PRESLEY JR FAMILY. I WAS GIVEN A VERY MOVING MILITARY TRIBUTE. IT WAS MY HONOR.

3 August 2007

I am not sure how all this stuff has happened. Mr. Presley Jr. the real deal son of the Late Mr. Presley was doing a sign autographic gig and the rest is history. I went into

A dream not able to grasp that I was discovered by him. However it was no dream. It all happened. Mr. Presley Jr. is absolutely delightful;. A true American entertainment in the delightful tradition of the Presley tradition.

4 August 2007

A very wicked young lady wiped my yellow folder given to me by Elvis Jr. This folder was an affirmation and significant to me. You can trust very few in America

8 August 2007

A very good dialogue with Deacon John today. The Lord is so good. How can you out give the Lord? You can't out give the Lord. I am still basking in the Glory of being

Invited into the Presley Family. Mr. Presley Jr. is such a good, and kind man. It is an honor to serve such a kind person.

9 AUGUST

Today it was the day of the Lord's touch as I preached on the Court Square. I am now the "Preacher of the Court Square". What a glorious day in the Lord.

I had a blast as I sang John Lennon's number on peace.

17 AUGUST 2007

The Yellow Jackets Sidney Football team played today. It was a very nice event.

28 AUGUST 2007

Great day at Shelby Oaks Golf Club. My 7 iron was hot on the golf range at 100 yrs. I should have stayed with the 7 iron because when I switched to my 3 wood my shots Were off center and wild.

6 SEPTEMBER 2007

Dan emailed me today. He is contacting Dave about getting together. It is great hearing from my son. I have slowed down. I've come down from being hypo manic for a few weeks.

So now I keep to myself and stay out of trouble. I am keeping my big mouth shut. I am focused on being stable and behaving myself in front of others. I am counting my blessings.

I do more reading now and less showing off in public. Mercedes says that I have come along way in one year. I try now to be the father that my sons would be proud of.

7 SEPTEMBER 2007

I have issues. This I know. I am not going to get down on myself. I have come a long way and I've got a long way to go. So what? I have sons that love me. This is all

I care about. I make mistakes. I learn from them. Theresa has the checkbook because I can't be trusted with it. All that matters is my sons. That is what I life for.

14 SEPTEMBER 2007

Got job thru CBS personnel service 3rd shift at a "bindery". Can't wait to start Sunday.

18 SEPTEMBER 2007

Production work is not for me. The 12 hour shifts killed me. When my back started to act up I bailed out. To deliver newspapers is more my style.

21 SEPTEMBER 2007

Depressed over my manic self. I sure wish I would leave people alone. I am staying home and keeping to myself.

23 SEPTEMBER 2007

All that matters is family. Theresa made dinner. My mood swings sometimes get the better of me. I seem to improve very slowly. All that matters is family.

My home is my castle. I see how foolish it is to run all over town playing a role that I am not. The best role is that of father. My issues will get better in time.

I will work towards a better self. I will win over all the stuff that brings me down.

29 SEPTEMBER 2007

Have worked with Theresa a week now delivering the town newspaper. We are productive and it sure beats depressive events. My mood swings are Now working themselves out. We have a job. We are productive and effective. Paid off cashland and tomorrow we are going to China Garden Buffet

For my birthday. Theresa is in charge of all fiscal issues since I can not be trusted with it.

2 OCTOBER 2007

The news job is working out fine. I am a productive worker

8 OCTOBER 2007

it's hard on me not hearing from my sons. They are productive and hard working and that is good. 2 years now and I have not seen them. Oh well maybe things will turn around.

14 OCTOBER 2007

is there any worst cancer than divorce? Old pictures and letters and cards of a love that failed. Divorce is worst than axe murder of the heart. It is a twisted form of emotional pain. I must live with this pain and learn for it. My heart bleeds from this pain. My stability must come first. That stability is prime. If I fail then all is lost. I have me. That which endures is primal to my emotional health

8 NOVEMBER 2007

Depression has set in. Sometimes I lie in bed all day. Lately I am reading Dean Koontz. He is a very good read. Daniel my son has emailed me. I read and that helps me heal

9 November 2007

I have been doing better with depression. I get up and read. Mom got hurt with the car. Maryann is now driving. Theresa and I are talking about seeing Brant Lake next summer.

21 November 2007

Maryann went manic again and is now on a psych ward. Mom didn't know who I was on the phone tonight. I long for the Thanksgivings of old. It's just Theresa and I.

Thursday is Thanksgiving. Thank God I have Theresa. Daniel has been emailing me more and I really love it. Thank God for Theresa

23 November 2007

Daniel called. It was delightful to hear from him. Today is a great day now that I heard from my son.

24 November 2007

Thank God for Theresa. She is my best friend

28 November 2007

Mom has invited Theresa and I for Christmas. She called twice not knowing she had already called. She is even talking about cooking a turkey. We are now figuring out the cost of this 660 mile trip. It's going to be 10 hours so we will have to stay at a hotel and break it up.

1 December 2007

Mom is paying for our Trip to New York for Christmas. She is delightful. She wants Theresa, and Maryann and I for the holiday. Her hearing is getting worst. She wont use the new phone system that would help her. She like the old phone. It's a 1400 miles round trip. 10 hrs one way. Today we brought car stuff for the trip. It's going to be a wonderful Christmas.

The days of the big dinners at Mom's is out. Time has passed and we are all passing thru this life. My family is very dysfunctional

2 DECEMBER 2007

I am most happy with Mom. She has always been on my side. Dad was a nazi prick but mom was the source of my love and faith in God. She is a good women like Theresa.

Today I am delighted to realize my many blessings. I no longer reside at the Salvation Army Booth House in Dayton Ohio. The apartment is wonderful and next year I hope to rent a house with Theresa and get her stuff out of storage. I am blessed with Dan and Dave. God is good. Life is good.

6 DECEMBER 2007

Mom has her good days and bad days. We hope to have a nice Christmas together with Maryann. I would be nice to be home for the Holidays. I write Mom every day

DECEMBER 2007

Mom is very excited to see us for Christmas. Maryann gets out of psych ward Friday. This will be a good Christmas. Theresa is baking an apple pie and Mom a turkey

DECEMBER 2007

I have been reading my medical records from Hampton Virginia VA. God was I sick. The police would be bringing me in to the psych ward over and over. I was totally out of my mind. Things were bad and Piper wasn't helping me by calling the police all the time. Somehow I feel blessed now that I am stable and have a good girl in my life. Theresa is wonderful. The VA showed up today and gave Theresa power as my payee of my VA check. This is good. I have proved to myself that I can not be trusted with money. I thank God for my peace of mind. Daniel has been emailing me. Today at the stores as I passed the Christmas Salvation Army people I was reminded of my stay at the Dayton Booth House. Thank God I am not longer there. Life is good. God is good. Maryann will be with us for Christmas. Mom is so excited to meet Theresa.

December 2007

I have not been hypo manic since September. No delusions. I guess its best that Theresa is now my payee. I really messed up the money. The Ron Paul sign wave is today at the Court Square. This is cool. I pray he wins. A balanced stable life has a lot to offer me. Oh yes living on the edge did too. The results of manic are hard to live with. Sometimes I still wonder what has become of my daughter. Pieper was so unstable that she made the mess of losing our daughter to the state. Thank God that chapter of my life is over. I have a good life now. I am very happy to not have manic events in my life now. Back in 1993 and 1994 the police was always driving me back to the VA psych ward. I was a very sick pup. I enjoy my Catholic faith. I has supported me thru the hell of psychosis. I must try to get to confession soon. It has been awhile.

December 2007

Spider broke up with Maryann for her girlfriend. It's the same old story. You never will meet someone who is good for you in a bar. She never learns. I stopped the bar scene long ago. I wasted a lot of money in bars. I used to go to strip joints. What a waste. Today I will go to confession. I love Holy Angels. I have much to thank God for. I don't really know if Maryann has learned her lesson. I am afraid she will find herself in a group home like me. I spent 5 years at Veterans House. 1 year in my own apartment with an alcoholic. I have gone so well this last year. My faith in God has been prime. Today I will confess how I abuse women verbally and emotionally. This is why I am divorced. I didn't do much better with my second wife Yvonne. I have much to learn. Thank God I have settled down. I will make a good confession. My soul will be clean. I must always be a where that heaven is my home. Dad was afraid to die. I wont go out that way. I hope to die in my home with my children. I miss my kids. Thank God I still have some contact with them. It's snowing today. Hopefully Tuesday when we leave for New York the drive will be safe and sound. I love my mother. She has always been good to me. I will be such a blessing to see her again. Maryann just doesn't get it. She is so lonely without a man in her life. She wont leave the bar scene alone. Back in 1993 I was living on a camp ground. I was homeless. God has given me a great women to help me and a wonderful apartment. My life is full of blessings. Divorce came close to destroying me. But now I am whole and solid. I shall leave for confession now.

Reflection: My version of faith is not to convert the world but save myself from me. I have it in for myself. I have been blessed with family, dysfunctional or not. It is my belief that God gave me Theresa. My life is now balanced and stable, Thank God. I look forward to a wonderful Christmas with Mom and Maryann. I know my faith reflects my mother's faith in God.

I shall not die depressed and sad like my father did. I shall live and die in my faith. The church to me is the community of faithful. This community reflects the peace and joy of Christ.

I refuse the bar scene. I refuse to feel the need to save the world. How I treat others reflects my inner faith. I have no desire of preaching on the Court Square. Those days are over. Thank God for that. I also see no reason to give up on golf just because I cant hit the ball 200 yards. So what. I spent a lot of money on my clubs. What is the problem with Theresa and I taking lessons together? I must practice, practice, and practice. I love the game. Its going to take time. My swing is going to need a lot of work. Another issue is that it isn't that important that I be a low handicap right now. I must give myself time to work on my game..

29 DECEMBER 2007

On the trip out to New York we got lost on route 30. we got hung up in traffic on the Throgs Neck bridge. We had a good time but it is nice to be home. Mom's short term memory is worst. The dogs run the house and Mom is not looking out for her best interest. That is what she wants. Nickie her nurse is great. It is hard to see Moms health decline.

I enjoy being home. That is my life. I am looking out for my wellness.

31 DECEMBER 2007

Daniel has been emailing me. It's been great hearing from him. I've settled down a lot lately. Tonight is Pondersoda. I love steak. I will read Thomas Merton for the New Years. Sometimes at night of dream of the old days with Dorothy. Today I will reflect upon all my blessings. I live in a wonderful 2 bedroom with Theresa. My son Daniel emails me. I have stabilized and no longer give money away. Yes, Theresa is my payee. However I earned that. My faith in the Lord continues. I wish I could do more for my Mothers failing health issues. My spirit awakens to the center of my faith in Christ. Confession is my friend. Fr Patrick is such a God

Send. In a few hours the New Year of 2008 will be here. God fills my soul with the wind of his blessings. Ron Paul is the only congressman that I feel is serving the issues needed for a free America. May the God of your choice bless you.

5 JANUARY 2008

Dream of Brant Lake, Mom, Doug, with a Elite Guard twist. Mom is dying as we all are up at Brant Lake. I am talking to Mom on the phone. Doug is inviting her to Brant Lake for a $5,000 vacation. Then the Elite Guard shows up for a control issue. When will I forget what happened so long ago? How long will it haunt me? I live a good life now. I will go to confession today. Fr Patrick is totally cool. I must get cleaned up now. Will chat later.

6 JANUARY 2008

Fr Patrick tells me I am a spiritual person. What I remember was how broken I was. At Norfolk Naval Base, I had no money so I would eat the left over pizza that others had not eaten. Some guys left salt and peppered pizza for me and got a big laugh. Christmas was horrid. Today I have Theresa. I have this computer. I have my car. Much more than I did when I was sleeping in the woods to see my sons. The primal thing in my life is that I am now stable. I am very happy with what I have. No, not much compared to Douglas but better than past lost years. When I remember Salvation Army Booth House it seems like a dream. But I was there. Homeless and Forgotten, Christ has saved me. The worst of the forgotten years was walking late at night in Danville Virginia. Some tuff blacks hit me from behind as I hit the guard rail of a bridge. If I had gone over that bridge I would be dead now. On Monday I will take myself out to Outback Steakhouse. I will reward myself with a delightful steak lunch. Gone are the homeless years. I may not have much but I am well and I will stay well.

I read Tom Clancy now. I enjoy reading. When the weather breaks I will go out for walks.

7 JANUARY 2008

I took my Christmas money and went to a poplar bar and grill for a steak dinner. Ponderosa was much better and less expensive. I was paying for 20 something staff and hip interior. At 57 I was out of place. The portions were small. The steak just didn't match Ponderosa. I will shop Sidney Food town for a steak that Theresa can grill at home. In a few short years I will be 60 years old. I hope to be a better 60 and more stable 60 than I am now. I was looking at the photo album. I have no idea where the time has gone. I should have gone to the Outback steak house. I have much to be thankful for. I need to take better care of me. I still dream of Dorothy and Cris. Those are part of the lost years. On Saturday I will go to confession again. I will listen to the wise words of Fr Patrick. I suppose that the days of sleeping in the men's room on base to see my sons are finally over. What a life. Today I had a street person banging on my door asking for money that I don't have to give him. Thank God he went away. It's the same old story. Kevin trying to correct the streets with God on his side. Thank God I have a warm house to sleep in. I remember sleeping in enlisted barracks at Langley Virginia. I was homeless and checking out and in everyday. I must be thankful for all that God has done. I now will drink tea and read Clancy. I will praise my God for a warm house.

13 JANUARY 2008

I have been depressed lately. Cant get out of bed. I must get up and read Tom Clancy. I spent all of yesterday in bed. That must go. Oh well. Such is life in the big city.

Another dream of Dorothy. I guess I will never get over her.

I messed up my life. Sometimes I wonder what life would be like still married to Dot. I could have taken care of

Dan and Dave. Cris was a big mistake. The night I took her to dinner I lied to Dot. I told Dot I was working. That dinner cost me a marriage. The following years were a horrid nightmare. But I was the cause of it. I should have been a better father and husband. If the divorce didn't happen perhaps the boys and I would be closer. But you must work with what your deal. Perhaps if I remember living downtown Dayton and working at 4am unloading trucks for a living. Perhaps I will better enjoy today. The boys came over to my room and my food was out on the window. How sad. When the boys were young Dot would bring them to me. Living in a tent was also a sad day. What a life. Jesus is so very kind to me. I will read more Clancy. I am most glad for my church. I find such peace there. Fr Patrick is so very kind to me. I should have never let Cris use me as she did. You cant buy love. Boy, did I have to learn that the hard way. So many years lost. Well God does heal. I need to relax my mind. It must be quieted. Zen Mediation would help. Tai Chi would also be helpful.

Theresa helped me write a great letter to WPAFB. She writes so well. I hope I hear something. Her letter was to the point and on target. I re-read an old letter to Base Legal. It sounded nutz. My mind needs to settle down and write normal. I don't know normal. Normal is boring.

JANUARY 2008

Woke up to stupid dreams. I am going for social security disability again. I am not giving up. I want what I am entitled too. I have been very ill. I want what is expected. I have suffered due to manic psychosis. The stupid people are trying to deny me what I am entitled too. I am not giving up. Mr.

Smith served me well. I wrote a letter to the editor. This is a new year. I will stay well and stable. I don't seem to get into reading lately. I am staying out of bed. My money crush is something that I must accept. I must learn how to save money. I really messed up last year. It's going to take sometime to get right.

15 JANUARY 2008

I don't drink alcohol and I resent social security saying if I were sober I could work. I am going to fight for my justice.

21 JANUARY 2008

I drove Dean to appointments. I had steak at Ponderosa It was great. I am going to read my book.

22 January 2008

A long email from Dan. He is working hard. He doesn't like his job. Health Ledger is dead at 28. What a loss.

25 January 2008

Reading a novel about the streets. It seems like a dream. Giving blood for a sandwich. St Vincent's Hotel for the homeless. Did it really happen to me? Yes it did. How did I survive?

Just saw a "Knight's Tale". Heath Ledger at his best. All my life I wanted to be someone. To be noticed and important and if this act would happen, then my Father's emotional abuse when I was young would be over. I want to be famous and this act I have quested since youth. Today I was offered a job snowplowing the sidewalk. I am someone. I am a survivor just like Fr Patrick says I am. My father is dead. My mother is also going to die sometime coming. I have me. I must make the best of today. It is all that I have.

26 JANUARY 2008

A dream of the Elite Guard. The General's all impressed with my military bearing. My father there. All this tech equipment. Bags of personal stuff to ship out. I so much wanted to be noticed. All of that now gone. Its history. I have me. I will read.

28 JANUARY 2008

I find it affirming that the local paper has printed my letters to the editor. Depression is still a big part of my day. I have heard nothing from my letters to WPAFB

My disorder is most difficult. My dreams haunt me at night. Oh Lord dear God, save me from me. I missed confession with Fr Patrick. How sad.

30 JANUARY 2008

Thank God for my stable home. It's fridge outside today. Tomorrow is the day I file with social security disability. I just put all the paperwork together. I spent 5 years at Veteran's House. Group Homes are not cool. There is always a problem. 1998 July – Jan 2003. I don't know how I did it. I still seek out attention. Maybe that's why I write so much to the Editor of the local paper. I really blew my interview with the VA. As usual I wasn't thinking of what I was saying. I really did a number on myself. I got out of bed early today and went to the Alcove. I had my regular steak and eggs. The people of this town just pretend that I don't exist. I really don't care.

31 JANUARY 2008

Well I did a good job today filing for social security disability. It was my best work. Steak dinner tonight. Oh boy. Snow tonight. Will be doing walks. I haven't seen Dan and Dave since Ponderosa 2005. Meanwhile my Cebu family calls me daddy. I need a family. I don't have one. I also need a bank account

2 FEBRUARY 2008

I love talking with Belona. She is so cute. I would love to visit Cebu. This is going to that some planning

9 FEBRUARY 2008

It's a Sunday Parade with Dorothy and kids. I'm dressed in my Elite Guard Dress Uniform. I ask my Commander for my weapon. He says sure but try to be here at 8am next time. I drop a quarter on the floor and pick up my 38 Special Smith and Wesson. Again dreams of the Air Force visit me. I got a very nice letter from Sidney Food Town today.

11 FEBRUARY 2008

Lord, I thank you for my sons. I thank you for my life. My work is too serve you in worship. I ask not anything from you except your constant love. Mold me into your spirit oh Lord. In the Confessional let me pour out my spirit and soul. Oh Lord Dear God thank you for Father Patrick. Such a wonderful priest.

My father Arthur jealous of his own son planed my madness. Now I know my way home

12 FEBRUARY 2008

All my life Lord I just wanted to gain my father affirmation. To be my father's hero. I will be the best Catholic I can at Holy Angel's and I will love my sons.

13 February 2008

I am naked dressing with Cris. We are married. Man, what a weird dream

17 February 2008

Today I went to Mass. It was delightful

18 February 2008

I don't like me very much. I don't know where I learned to dislike me. I have been looking at Dad's picture on my desktop. I still love the old bastard. He sure could be mean. But he loved me in his own twisted way. He was a handsome man. Cheap as hell. He mistreated Mom most of their life. He didn't like him either. He loved to yell. I wonder where he is. Heaven or Hell. He did see a priest before he died. Thank God for that. Theresa is my little doll. She is very cute. She sure is doing a great job as my custodian. I have money in the bank. Praise God for that. All the bills are paid on time. Everything is balanced to the penny. It's a job being done right. I just poured sugar soda down the drain. I have been drinking way too much sugar and not taking my insulin. Not good at all. Confession with Fr. Patrick going very well indeed. He is quite kind to me. I think the coldest thing that Dad did was invite me to Disneyland and then drop me off alone. It sucked. All those family's and kids having a great time and I was all alone. Dad was an angry man. Not a happy camper. Mom is alone now. It's a good thing that Maryann is with her.

Dear Dad,
I miss you very much. I am sorry we didn't do more stuff together. Theresa is doing a very good job as my custodian. The checkbook is balanced to the penny. I am blessed to have her. So how is heaven? What's your email address up there.

What's heaven like Dad? I guess I will have to wait till I get there.

I hear you had Last Rites. Did you make a good confession? We all love and miss you. All my life I wanted your affirmation Dad. Now you are with Jesus in Heaven. I will never talk to you again in this life.

I remember carrying your casket at church. The church bells were so loud. Someday in the future I will join you in heaven. Maybe we could play some golf with St Peter

19 FEBRUARY 2008

Well social security says a decision has been made and a letter is in the mail. I sure hope so. Dr Walters left a very nice message. At least he is on my side. I fear I have been rejected again. I will get my medical records back. I am bored with my life. I wish to have social security to pay off my debt.

20 FEBRUARY 2008

Praise God for Rick the homeless man. I could be Rick. Thank God I have a warm home. Thank God I have Theresa. I count my blessings. It's very cold and bitter out and Rick is out there with no place to go.

26 FEBRUARY 2008

The dreams of my sons as little boys continues. I miss my sons. I haven't heard a word from David in over 2 years. Daniel emails me. Dear Lord I know you are in charge of my life. I look forward to confession on Saturday and Mass. Lord help me accept all that has happened in my life. I never asked for Bipolar disorder. I wish to hear from my sons.

29 FEBRUARY 2008

It's 3:30am and I am awake. Today I see the VA Dayton Dentist. I really don't look after myself. I should brush my teeth everyday and take insulin. I don't like me and I take it out on myself. Look at how the Lord loves me! I have such a good life compared to the streets. Why don't I like me? I don't get it. My teeth show my abuse. My medical records reflect my dental abuse. So why am I still doing this to myself?

Thank God I don't drink. Now that would be a problem. Deacon John was so kind to me the other day. What would I do without Deacon John and Father Patrick? Lord somehow help me to like me and take better care of myself. I hope to see my sons soon. I haven't seen them since Nov 05. That's just the way it is.

1 MARCH 2008

I slept in today to catch up on yesterday. We just ordered Papa john's Pizza. I love my new shoes. My stomach feels much better today. Dear Lord please help me take better care of me. Help me like myself. I love my apartment. I know that with your help dear Lord I can do better.

2 MARCH 2008

Dear Lord thank you for Theresa. She helps me cope. Thank you for my car and all the things you have given me. Dear Lord I am so thankful that I am not in jail. I hated jail. 92 days for sending flowers. Thank you Lord for the love of Theresa.

6 MARCH 2008

Dear Dorothy,
You were the best ex-wife I ever had. I failed as a husband and father. There is little I can do about that. You have told

me you wish to have nothing to do with me. This is very sad. Divorce is very sad. I hate divorce. It kills the family like axe murder of the heart. I wish we could be friends but that is not what you wish. I wish I could re-write my life. It would be filled with my family. I would be a good father and they would show their love for me. As it now I have not heard a word from David in over 2 years. This sucks. Today I will reward myself with steak dinner at Ponderosa. I no longer live the streets. That part of my life is over. Divorce is sarcoma. It is cancer. It kills. Oh, how I wish I could re do my life. No, Bipolar disorder and no divorce. How delightful that would be

13 MARCH 2008

Before the entire command I am asking to contact the 4 star on phone. Trained police dogs show up and my picture is taking with the command Chaplin who asked my name. Nice dream

22 MARCH 2008

Islam VIP has heart condition and I am taking care of him at important conference. This was a nice dream.

23 MARCH 2008

A wonderful Easter Sunday Mass. God is good.

27 MARCH 2008

Lord, thank you for Theresa. Life is good. I look forward to confession. Protect my son David. I have not heard a word from him. Such is life.

28 March 2008

Dear Father,
You have been dead a year. I miss you very much. I wish we had many more good times together than we did. Dad, you were hard on me. But in your own twisted way you loved me. I will play golf for you. Golf was a gift that you gave to me. We never played a game. Why did you leave me alone at Disneyland? It was so sad to see all the other family's. I love you Dad. I am so sorry we had hard times together.

31 March 2008

Daniel emailed me today. It was so nice to hear from him. Thank God that he does keep me posted. I was looking at his baby pictures. Where does the time go? I am hoping for a golf outing. A three some. Dan, Dave, and I. Sounds cool to me. It's been years since we have played together. I love the game just wish I was better at it. It takes time to learn the stroke. Will love to hit the links. Oh well that's life.

17 April 2008

I miss dad. I watched Master and Commander last night thinking of him. We saw that film together. I miss Dad. It was so sad we had so few moments together. What an angry man. He was forever having fights. Well I hope he is at peace now. Just because he was not a happy camper doesn't mean that I have too be. Mom and Maryann are coming out this summer and Daniel wants to meet them. Cool.

20 April 2008

Oh Lord I am so thankful for Theresa and our apartment. I am no longer homeless thank God. Dear Lord Mom is coming out this summer. Oh that will be great. Daniel will be there plus all our friends. How delightful. God is Good.

28 APRIL 2008

Maryann is taking such good care of Mom. They go to restaurants together. Maryann has really settled down. I really love my sister. I am so glad she is well.

29 APRIL 2008

The dreams of babysitting my boys and seeing Dorothy keep rolling along. It so sad to wake up

30 APRIL 2008

A dream of a golf game with Dad but Dad is dead. Very weird dream. I see Audrey today. We are going to a prayer meeting. I love her dearly. She has always been a source of kindness and goodness. She even loaned me $4,000 which I paid back.

6 MAY 2008

Daniel is talking Air Force Reserves. He is a man now. He is no longer a boy. He must follow his dream. He will make the right choice. I fear him going to the front lines and coming home in a box

7 MAY 2008

Dear Dad,
You have been dead over a year now. I miss you. I guess you know about Daniel talking Air Force Reserves. Do you get my email in heaven? I wont forget your funeral. Carrying your casket was a trip.

Well we have savings in the bank thanks to Theresa. I have never had savings like this. She is a doll.

Just saw a great golf movie on DVD. Theresa bought it for me. All I have to do is find my swing. I will do just that.

9 MAY 2008

This is the best. Money in the bank. A good car running fine. Clean clothes. Nice shoes. I could get used to this. Theresa is very good for me. I should treat her better. I guess I am high maintenance

16 MAY 2008

Lost my golf swing. Can't hit my wood's. Hitting my 7 iron off a tee.

28 MAY 2008

Totally out of shape and not taking meds as prescribed. I should be taking care of myself. I am not.

My diabetes is out of control. Not taking insulin shots. Chronic indigestion. Sleep all day

29 MAY 2008

Up at 5am. Ate at the Alcove. Went to 7:00am Mass.

30 MAY 2008

Found my swing on the pitching wedge. Arrow shots 125 yards with nice arc. I am going to learn this game of golf and make Dad proud

31 MAY 2008

Dear Dad,
What's heaven like Dad? Are you at peace? I sure do hope so. I'm still playing golf. I guess you know that. I miss you Dad. I wish we could have played golf together. Oh well, can't get it all. Theresa and I are together. She is wonderful

1 JUNE 2008

As I sip my one bottle of Light Corona a week on the porch I reflect the goodness of life. How delightful this stable wellness that I now enjoy. Thanks to Theresa money in the bank and 2 credit card paid off. How oh Lord you love me well.

4 JUNE 2008

Great day for a golf lesson. I am hitting my 6 iron. Got some great shots today

10 JUNE 2008

Really want to nail my 3 wood. It's going to take some practice to get this right. Actually it will take years to learn the game. I have a problem with balance. I step off balance. Right now I am happy with 150 yards. That's my best right now.

17 JUNE 2008

Daniel called Father's Day. Got caught up on Dan and Dave. Really great phone call. Best father's day ever.

24 JUNE 2008

Dear Dad you have been dead since last 20 March 07. I will never see you again. I miss you very much. How I wish we were closer in the living years. I am glad for what we had. I am glad you cried on the phone. My dysfunction was learned from you. God is good. How I delight in the Lord. Theresa is taking good care of me Dad.

9 JULY 2008

I remain very depressed over my family issue. Haven't seen my sons in over 3 yrs. It is most sad.

23 July 2008

I had the most profound dream of teaching poetry.

30 July 2008

What I need to know is that I AM SEEING MY SONS NEXT MONTH. That is all I need to know. I must let them life their life and stop asking them to see me. They love me and wish to see me. That is all I need to know. Next I must focus on my spiritual life. Confession and Mass. Next I must resume Golf. Focus on my short game. I need the exercise. Golf is fun. I may not be very good but I can focus on my short game and improve. Let's face it I will never hit the drive 300 yards. So What!.

31 July 2008

Dear Lord I thank you for another day of wellness. I thank you for Theresa and my sons. Help me to always count my blessings. Watch over me today dear Lord and guide my way in light of the faith my mother has shown me.

6 August 2008

My beloved sons will be at China Garden Buffet in a week from now. Mom and Maryann will be there as well as Dot, Daniel, and David. It will be great seeing my sons. Family is family

8 August 2008

I thank you Dear Lord for the gift of life. Social Security Mental Status Exam went very well. After an hour and ½ Dr Allen had taken a narrative of my life. In a few weeks I should hear the results. I am looking forward to seeing my sons on Wednesday. 3 yrs has passed since I have seen them. Dear

Lord I am blessed because of you. Gone are the days I was homeless. Gone are the days I was in jail for disturbing the peace. Gone is last summer when I was hypo manic. I will end my quest for food in restaurants that are costly. In the end I shall die in the faith that I learned from my mother. Praise God for life is good. God is good and deserving of all our love and faith.

13 AUGUST 2008

Saw Dot, Dan, and David at China Garden Buffet and it was awesome. I am blessed with a delightful family. Took lots of photos. Thank you Lord for such a wonderful family. It was awesome being with them.

17 AUGUST 2008

Had a wonderful time at Jazz Night at In good Taste. The food was great. The jazz awesome. Mom was delightful.

20 AUGUST 2008

I think that when it comes down to it two things stand out. A good book, and prime rib. How I delight in the Outback Restaurant. Nobody has better Prime Rib than the Outback. I delight in such simple pleasure.

I am so blessed. How wonderful to have such a delightful family. My sons are pure joy. Life offers me a chance to see my sons over the upcoming holidays.

24 AUGUST 2008

I fail to understand why I neglect dental care. I now have a bad and painful tooth because of this. I fear it will be pulled. My whole life I have had poor dental health. How sad that this condition continues today

26 SEPTEMBER 2008

I have colon cancer. I went a week without food. Thank God I am eating again. I am in the care of our Lord. His will shall be done.

22 NOVEMBER 2008

I accept I have terminal cancer. Your will be done Lord

6 JANUARY 2009

Nothing I eat tastes the same as it did 17 September of the surgery. Oh Lord this be your will for me than let it be painless.

1 JANUARY 2009

It's a cold, cold, cold winter's night. I have an incision the size of the Great Wall of China and I'm told I have a couple of year's left to live. I am suppose to be happy about all of this? Lord why is all this happening to me?

26 JANUARY 2009

I am checking in to 7 South. I just want to get 8 hours of sleep. The nightmares are horrid. I am not trilled with the way cancer works. I am dying

28 JANUARY 2009

Dear Lord I wish to thank you for my angel Theresa. She is wonderful and I don't deserve her attention.

I leave this world in the love of family and friends. I couldn't ask for a better family.